END TIMES

IN A SNAP

Are You Ready?

Monoseta Burwell

End Times in a Snap

Trilogy Christian Publishers
A Wholly Owned Subsidiary of Trinity Broadcasting Network
2442 Michelle Drive Tustin, CA 92780

Trilogy Christian Publishing/TBN and colophon are trademarks of Trinity Broadcasting Network. For information about special discounts for bulk purchases, please contact Trilogy Christian Publishing.

Trilogy Disclaimer: The views and content expressed in this book are those of the author and may not necessarily reflect the views and doctrine of Trilogy Christian Publishing or the Trinity Broadcasting Network.

Manufactured in the United States of America
10 9 8 7 6 5 4 3 2 1
Library of Congress Cataloging-in-Publication Data is available.

ISBN: 978-1-63769-262-2
E-ISBN: 978-1-63769-263-9

PREFACE

People can sense that we are approaching the end of time. Quite a few have read the entire Bible and are watching and waiting for the last seven years to unfold. Many believe in the Rapture of the church (many do not) but cannot figure out where, or if, it falls in the last seven years of world history. Many people believe Jesus is coming back for the church but have no idea where the event fits in the apocalyptic and prophetic scriptures timeline. They have read the Bible from Genesis to Revelation (and you should) but cannot pin any of it down as it relates to the end of the world.

This book is a walk through the last seven years of the world. It will guide you as it brings the supporting scriptures together in one place at each step. You will be guided from the Rapture to the Millennial reign of Jesus Christ and to the new heaven and new earth.

It is my desire to make this so straight forward and clear that if you were in the last seven years, you could pick this book up, know where you are, understand what is going on and what to expect next. Most importantly you will recognize just how impossible being in the Tribulation really is. Captured in a one world government, it becomes like hell on earth with everyone held captive by Satan and his deceivers the antichrist and the false prophet. There is only one way out. His Name is Jesus Christ.

Neither is there salvation in any other: for there is none other name under heaven given among men, whereby we must be saved.

—Acts 4:12 (KJV)

ACKNOWLEDGEMENTS

To Pastor Bruce D. Burwell, my husband, and to Chera M Burwell, my daughter, both of whom gave me love, space, and time to complete this work. A special thank you to Chera for her help with all grammar, computer, and software questions.

TABLE OF CONTENTS

PROLOGUE

God Loves Us All

> We love Him, because He first loved us.
> —1 John 4:19 (KJV)

It is important to understand we live in the world that was corrupted after Adam and Eve disobeyed God and let sin enter it. The end-time is not coming because God is mad at us. The end of this world as we know it, is coming because God loves us and wants us to live in the world that He designed for us. Yes, God loves us. He created us. He gave us the plans that we consider the desires of our heart. Your mother and father conceived you, but God formed you and set His plans for success in your heart (Jeremiah 1:5). Seeking the God of the plan would allow or would have allowed you to find out the plan, and fulfill the plan (Luke 11:9, Revelation 3:20).

God loved Adam. Adam was created in God's own image and given dominion over everything on the earth (Genesis 1:26-28).

[26] And God said, 'Let us make man in our image, after our likeness: and let them have dominion over the fish of the sea, and over the

> fowl of the air, and over the cattle, and over
> all the earth, and over every creeping thing
> that creepeth upon the earth.'
>
> ²⁷ So God created man in his own image,
> in the image of God created he him; male
> and female created he them.
>
> ²⁸ And God blessed them, and God said
> unto them, 'Be fruitful, and multiply, and re-
> plenish the earth, and subdue it: and have
> dominion over the fish of the sea, and over
> the fowl of the air, and over every living thing
> that moveth upon the earth.'
>
> —Genesis 1:26-28 (KJV)

God created a garden filled with trees that were attrac-
tive, and that were for food. Also, along with the trees in
the garden were gold and precious stones. The garden was
named Eden. Adam was to dress it and keep it (Genesis
2:9-15). God like all good fathers, gave Adam the "do's and
don'ts" of the garden.

> ¹⁶ And the LORD God commanded the man,
> saying, 'Of every tree of the garden thou
> mayest freely eat:
>
> ¹⁷ But of the tree of the knowledge of good
> and evil, thou shalt not eat of it: for in the day
> that thou eatest thereof thou shalt surely die.'

¹⁸ And the LORD God said, 'It is not good that the man should be alone; I will make him an help meet for him.'

—Genesis 2:16-18 (KJV)

He could eat of any of the thousands of trees in the garden. But the one tree of the knowledge of good and evil Adam should not eat. God did not say he could not, but that Adam should not. Then God told Adam why he should not eat of the tree in Genesis 2:17, because he would surely die. When God gives instructions, even to us, it is not to hurt us, but the instructions are to help us, like Adam, because He loves us, more than we could ever know, or understand. God loves us with an everlasting love (Jeremiah 31:3). God still loves us when we make mistakes. He may correct us, but He still loves us, because He is a Good Father.

In Genesis 2:18 the Lord God says that Adam being alone is not good and so a help meet was going to be made also. I cannot think of a better gift to Adam, than to receive a woman to help him. That was true love. If given a choice, if you ask any real man stranded on an island would he choose an aspirin or a woman, he will choose the woman. Forget the aspirin.

But before the woman, God does something utterly amazing, just picture it.

¹⁹ And out of the ground the LORD God formed every beast of the field, and every fowl of the air; and brought them unto Adam to see what he would call them: and whatso-

ever Adam called every living creature, that was the name thereof.

²⁰ And Adam gave names to all cattle, and to the fowl of the air, and to every beast of the field; but for Adam there was not found an help meet for him.

²¹ And the LORD God caused a deep sleep to fall upon Adam, and he slept: and he took one of his ribs, and closed up the flesh instead thereof;

²² And the rib, which the LORD God had taken from man, made he a woman, and brought her unto the man.

²³ And Adam said, 'This is now bone of my bones, and flesh of my flesh: she shall be called Woman, because she was taken out of Man.'

—Genesis 2:19-23 (KJV)

If you were Adam, can you even picture the animals and birds being created from the dust of the earth and being brought to you to be named? How exciting is that? So much for the age-old question, "Which came first, the chicken or the egg?" The chicken came first.

Then you go to sleep, and God takes your rib, makes the most beautiful woman ever and brings her to you, performing the first wedding ceremony. The love of God is just evident everywhere and in everything in the creation story. By Genesis 3:1 the enemy of God and man (to get back at

God), Satan has indwelled the serpent and set Eve up for the fall. She eats of the tree of knowledge of good and evil and gives to Adam to eat. Death is separation from God. So now they are separated from their creator who loves them. The precious dominion over the world that Adam had is now transferred to Satan by that act of disobedience. Satan, who wanted to defeat God and take His place, is rejoicing over winning this battle. Satan, whose plan for Adam and all mankind for that matter, was then and even today, to steal, kill and destroy man. Satan has one major victory under his belt. That victory affected the course of history of the world, even to today. Satan probably thought it was a fatal blow, but God.

---

⁹ Remember the former things of old: for I am God, and there is none else; I am God, and there is none like me,

¹⁰ Declaring the end from the beginning, and from ancient times the things that are not yet done, saying, My counsel shall stand, and I will do all my pleasure.

—Isaiah 46:9-10 (KJV)

God, who was not taken by surprise, since He knows the end from the beginning, already had a plan. God's plan basically was and is that two things were going to happen:

1. God is going to receive a family of many sons and daughters of every race, color, and ethnic group for the Kingdom of God, and Sa-

tan, who was Lucifer in heaven, is going to get what he deserves.

2. Lucifer (Ezekiel 28:14-15), son of the morning (Isaiah 14:12-16), who started a war against God in heaven along with 2/3rds of the angels who followed him, was cast down to earth (between Genesis 1:1 and 1:2) and to hell (Isaiah 14:9-11) and will end up in the lake of fire and brimstone (Revelation 20:10).

That was all God wanted for His beautiful, holy, creations Adam and Eve, was to be fruitful and multiply the way God had designed for them. God our Father gave them free will to worship Him and to make decisions for themselves. He did not want robots. They were God's first son and daughter. And of their own free will they believed Satan and were enticed to eat of the forbidden fruit. When they did that, in addition to being separated from God, they transferred Adam's dominion over the world to Satan and his kingdom of darkness. Satan became the god of the world.

So, when we think of the end of the world, we need to focus on the fact that this is not the world as designed by God for His children that He loves. This is the corrupted evil world of the devil Satan, the prince of darkness. God loves us and wants us to have the good, beautiful, loving world that He designed. A government designed with God first and with God's son at the helm. And we will have it again during the 1000-year Millennial Reign of Christ. Christ is called the second Adam (1 Corinthians 15:45-47).

The Tribulation is seven years long, followed by the Millennial Reign of Christ (this is the only time frame about the end that we know for sure).

We are in the last of the last days. It is much closer than when Jesus spoke of it over 2,000 years ago. So, keep reading because time is short, all the calendars are wrong. We do not know the day or the hour, but we continue to look and watch for Jesus (Matthew 24:42; 1 Peter 4:7).

CHAPTER 1

Time Is Short

For God so loved the world, that he gave his only begotten Son, that whosoever believeth in him should not perish, but have everlasting life.

—John 3:16 (KJV)

And as He sat upon the mount of Olives, the disciples came unto Him privately, saying, 'Tell us, when shall these things be? and what shall be the sign of thy coming, and of the end of the world?'

—Matthew 24: 3 (KJV)

What you must quickly understand is that we are nearing the end of time as we know it. God created time in the beginning:

---

¹ In the beginning God created the heaven and the earth.

² And the earth was without form, and void; and darkness was upon the face of the

---

> deep. And the Spirit of God moved upon the face of the waters.
>
> ³ And God said, 'Let there be light: and there was light.'
>
> ⁴ And God saw the light, that it was good: and God divided the light from the darkness.
>
> ⁵ And God called the light Day, and the darkness he called Night. And the evening and the morning were the first day.
>
> —Genesis 1:1-5 (KJV)

Genesis 1:5 says, "the evening and the morning were the first day." But God is different from us, He does everything from the end to the beginning. So, by Genesis 1:5 the end of time was already completed.

> ⁹ Remember the former things of old: for I am God, and there is none else; I am God, and there is none like me,
>
> ¹⁰ Declaring the end from the beginning, and from ancient times the things that are not yet done, saying, 'My counsel shall stand, and I will do all my pleasure.'
>
> —Isaiah 46:9-10 (KJV)

Look at Isaiah 46:9. God explains, "I am God, and there is none like me." God goes on in verse 10 to explain that He declares "the end from the beginning." As a matter of fact, Jesus, God's only begotten Son, was slain "from the foundation of the world," as you find in Revelation 13:8.

Monoseta Burwell

(Notice the Word says, "from the foundation of the world," not the earth.)

> And all that dwell upon the earth shall worship him, whose names are not written in the book of life of the Lamb slain from the foundation of the world.
>
> —Revelation 13:8 (KJV)

Not only was Jesus the Lamb of God, His only begotten Son, slain from the foundation of the world, but we were chosen before then as well (Ephesians 1:4).

> 3 Blessed be the God and Father of our Lord Jesus Christ, who hath blessed us with all spiritual blessings in heavenly places in Christ:
>
> 4 According as He hath chosen us in Him before the foundation of the world, that we should be holy and without blame before Him in love.
>
> —Ephesians 1:3-4 (KJV)

> But ye are a chosen generation, a royal priesthood, an holy nation, a peculiar people; that ye should shew forth the praises of him who hath called you out of darkness into his marvelous light.
>
> —1 Peter 2:9 (KJV)

We "are a chosen generation, a royal priesthood," many are called but "few are chosen" Matthew 22:14 tells us. Chosen before the foundation of the world, to be a royal priesthood, a holy nation in the world, and are set aside for the Kingdom of Heaven which is the Kingdom of God.

But time as we know it will come to an end. The scripture says God created the heavens and the earth and all that is in it, including man, in six days, and rested on the seventh day. The scriptures, at times, have more than one timeframe contained within it. Just like in the book of Isaiah when he speaks of the birth of Christ:

> For unto us a child is born, unto us a son is given: and the government shall be upon His shoulder: and His name shall be called Wonderful, Counsellor, The mighty God, The everlasting Father, The Prince of Peace.
> —Isaiah 9:6 (KJV)

"The government shall be upon his shoulder" occurs during the 1,000-year millennial reign of Christ after Armageddon. The beginning of the scripture occurs during the birth of Jesus.

> For a thousand years in thy sight are but as yesterday when it is past, and as a watch in the night.
> —Psalms 90:4 (KJV)

> But, beloved, be not ignorant of this one
> thing, that one day is with the Lord as a thou-
> sand years, and a thousand years as one day.
> —2 Peter 3:8 (KJV)

The first six days of the creation is also considered the first 6 thousand years of human time. The day of rest day, seven, is considered the 1000-year millennial reign of Christ. After the 1,000-year reign we have the New Heaven and New Earth created for eternity (Garcia 2014). There is a beautiful must-see chart in the book *Charting the End Times* named "The Complete Bible Prophecy Chart," that shows in detail eternity past and future, and the ages within the six thousand years of human history. (LaHaye and Ice, *Charting the End Times* 2001)

So where are we now? First, know that no calendar is completely accurate. But the Jewish calendar (which is the Hebrew calendar) is probably the closest one we have. It is year 5781 according to the Jewish calendar year for 2020-2021. We will never know the day or the hour, but if you subtract the current Jewish calendar year 5781 from 6000, there are 219 years remaining. Although it may not be exact, it tells you that we are in the last days. Time is short. So, you must be ready. There will be no time to get ready at the rapture when we who are in Christ are caught up in the clouds (1 Thessalonians 4:16-17). Jesus will not stand in the clouds and say, "The doors of the church are open. If you are not saved or sure you are saved and would like to accept me as Lord and Savior, come forward." No, that takes more than an instant. There will be no time to get ready, you must be ready. That means today is the day, now is the time for salvation.

$$\Omega$$

You can be saved or born again right now and be 100% sure that you are going to heaven. Do you remember John 3:16 from the beginning of this chapter?

> For God so loved the world, that he gave his only begotten Son, that whosoever believeth in him should not perish, but have everlasting life.
>
> —John 3:16 (KJV)

Jesus died on the cross so that the whole world would not perish but would be saved. You must understand that we are spirit beings. We live in this body and we possess a soul. Our soul is our mind, will and emotions. Wherever your spirit goes your soul goes with it. Your body has a lifespan and dies (this began when Adam and Eve sinned). Your spirit and soul exist after your body is gone. Believing in Jesus, as Lord and Savior, you become a child of God and this will allow your spirit and soul to have everlasting life and be saved.

The question is, *saved from what?* Saved from perishing with Satan and his Kingdom of Darkness and being eternally separated from God, which is death. You may ask, "Aren't I already a child of God?" "I'm a good person and

I never do anything wrong. Won't that get me in heaven?" I would like the answer to be yes. Unfortunately, Adam and Eve made a different choice for the human race. Even though God had warned Adam against what they did and told him the consequences. Adam had dominion over the whole world and with that sin, gave it away to Satan. Satan gained the dominion over the world we live in, became the father of the world, and the prince of darkness. The world is now a part of the kingdom of darkness. The default choice for everyone after the age of understanding is being a member of the kingdom of darkness and having Satan as their father. At that point everyone must actively choose to believe in and accept Jesus Christ as their Lord and Savior to be saved from the kingdom of darkness. They then become a child of God and become a part of the Kingdom of God, which is the Kingdom of Heaven.

This is the "Good News" of Jesus Christ, you can be 100% sure right now that you are saved and going to Heaven. First look at Romans 10: 9-10.

---

⁹ That if thou shalt confess with thy mouth the Lord Jesus, and shalt believe in thine heart that God hath raised him from the dead, thou shalt be saved.

¹⁰ For with the heart man believeth unto righteousness; and with the mouth confession is made unto salvation.

—Romans 10:9-10 (KJV)

So, say out loud the following prayer and believe in your heart of hearts (not just your mind) what you are saying (We pray to the Father in the Name of Jesus):

> Dear Heavenly Father:
>
> I believe in my heart and confess with my mouth that Jesus is the Lord of my Life. I believe Jesus died for my sins on the Cross. I believe in my heart that God raised Jesus from the dead and He is alive right now. Please forgive me of any sins that I have committed of thought, word, or deed. Jesus, come into my heart right now and save me. I believe I am, right now, saved. I am right now born again.
>
> In Jesus's Name I pray.
>
> Amen.

Now find a Bible-based church on Sunday so you can start renewing your mind according to the Word of God, from all the old way of thinking (Romans 12:2, Colossians 3:10, Ephesians 4:23). This is particularly important because you need to increase your faith in God. The more you read and hear the Word of God the more your faith in God will increase, Romans 10:17. You also want to know the truth. There is freedom in the truth, John 8:32. The scripture, the Word of God, is "the truth".

> So then faith cometh *(continually comes)* by hearing and hearing by the word of God.
> —Romans 10:17 (KJV)

> And ye shall know the truth, and the truth shall make you free.
>
> —John 8:32 (KJV)

Welcome to the family of God. The angels in heaven are rejoicing.

Ω

As I mentioned, scripture is the Word of God. Look at John 1:1-4.

> ¹ In the beginning was the Word, and the Word was with God, and the Word was God.
>
> ² The same was in the beginning with God.
>
> ³ All things were made by Him; and without Him was not any thing made that was made.
>
> ⁴ In Him was life; and the life was the light of men.
>
> —John 1:1-4 (KJV)

The Word of God is a living Word. The Word is Jesus's eternal name. The written Word can reveal truth from God, answers from God, and guidance from God when you read it. The written Word can impart knowledge from God that He has prepared for you for a particular moment in time. We call it revelation knowledge. As a new Christian, the book of John is a great place to start your reading of the Bible.

So, as we continue this study of the "End-Times In-A-Snap," let us look again at the words of John 3:16 and Genesis 8:22:

> For God so loved the world, that he gave his only begotten Son, that whosoever believeth in Him should not perish but have everlasting life.
>
> —John 3:16 (KJV)

> While the earth remaineth, seedtime and harvest, and cold and heat, and summer and winter, and day and night shall not cease.
>
> —Genesis 8:22 (KJV)

First, just know that God is greater than we are. He does not think like we think, His thoughts are greater. Look at this:

1. God gave His Son. Jesus was born of a virgin named Mary. Our bodies were designed in God's image such that God's child, Jesus, could be carried in a woman and born a 100% God and 100% man to be able to accomplish all that Jesus did for us.

2. God gave us the Holy Spirit to live inside our spirit. That means in that when God designed us in His image, we were designed to be able to receive the Spirit of God living inside us, which seals us until the day of redemption (Ephesians 1:13, 4:30).

3. God designed us to be spirit beings that live in a body and possess a soul which is our mind, will, and emotions. When we repent of our sin and accept Jesus as our Lord and Savior, Holy Spirit comes to live in us. Even though we were dead because of Adam's sin, we are born again, "re-gened" or regenerated, given eternal life and more. We were designed so that our soul will follow our spirit leaving our bodies to go back to the dust where it came from at creation.

Secondly, let us look at this another way:

1. God gave His son Jesus. Jesus was the seed. "As long as the earth remaineth there will be seedtime and harvest . . ." Genesis 8:22.

2. Jesus came to bring the Kingdom of God to people that would believe in Him. Holy Spirit would come to live in them. They would become sons and daughters of God. Jesus the seed of God has multiplied in every nation, all over the world.

3. When over time, everyone on earth has had the opportunity to hear the gospel of the Kingdom of God, the end will come (Matthew 24:14).

4. During the end is the harvest where the church will be "raptured" or caught up to meet Jesus in the clouds and taken to heaven. Jesus told a parable about this time when the wheat (the children of God) and the tare (the children of Satan) will be harvested.

> Let both grow together until the harvest: and in the time of harvest I will say to the reapers, Gather ye together first the tares, and bind them in bundles to burn them: but gather the wheat into my barn.
>
> —Matthew 13:30 (KJV)

In the next chapter, and those following, you will find a concise study of the end times. That is why the title is "End-Times In-A-Snap." The subject of each chapter following will be found in one of the three major events of the "End-Times."

1. *In the Twinkling of an Eye*: The 7-year timetable begins; the Church is gone and what is

happening on earth. It includes what we do now while we wait. This is the 7-year period known as the "Tribulation," the catching away of the saints, by most Christians.

2. *The last 3 ½ years begins.* The abomination of desolation: The antichrist stands in the rebuild Temple and says he is God, and it is the start of the last 3 ½ years, called the Great Tribulation; What is happening now that everything is worse?

3. *God Keeps His Promises:* The second coming of Jesus Christ and Armageddon.

4. *And the Government shall be upon His Shoulder:* The Millennial Reign of Christ.

Ω

A picture is worth a thousand words. So, I recommend the following movies:

1. "Left Behind, The Movie" (LaHaye, Jenkins and McElroy, Left Behind The Movie 2000)

2. "Left Behind II Tribulation Force" (Lalonde and Patus 2002)

3. "Megiddo: The Omega Code 2" (Stephan Blinn 2001, Stephan Blinn 2001), Satan bows his knee in this movie.

CHAPTER 2

In the Twinkling of an Eye

---

⁵¹ Behold, I shew you a mystery; We shall not all sleep, but we shall all be changed,

⁵² In a moment, in the twinkling of an eye, at the last trump: for the trumpet shall sound, and the dead shall be raised incorruptible, and we shall be changed.

⁵³ For this corruptible must put on incorruption, and this mortal must put on immortality.

—1 Corinthians 15:51-53 (KJV)

---

¹⁷ Then we which are alive and remain shall be caught up together with them in the clouds, to meet the Lord in the air: and so shall we ever be with the Lord.

¹⁸ Wherefore comfort one another with these words.

—1 Thessalonians 4:17-18 (KJV)

The Tribulation Is Ushered In

The last trumpet sounds. The catching away of the saints

occurs. In a twinkling of an eye, a moment, what a short period of time… No time to say goodbye to earthly friends, but a mystery unfolds, and we can meet the Lord, say hello to the Lord, our friend Jesus. How amazing! All this will happen in the air, in the clouds. From that point forward and into eternity we will be with the Lord.

> Behold, I shew you a mystery.
> —1 Corinthians 15: 51 (KJV)

This is why there are so many questions. It is a mystery. The end-time is one of the mysteries. A mystery is a secret. In the Greek, the word mystery means silence until initiation into religious rites. The initiation is when you are saved or born again. Even the numbers in this very scripture is part of the mystery, and only scratches the surface of the lengths God will go to reveal to His sons and daughters, revelation knowledge hidden just for them.

Let me explain some of the mystery of the numbers. The chapter is 15. 5 times 3 equal the number 15. 5 is the number of grace (Ephesians 2:8, For by grace are ye saved through faith; and that not of yourselves: it is the gift of God. KJV). 3 is the number of divine perfection. And so, the number 15 represents those things performed by the power of divine grace, which is carried out by the Holy Spirit, the power (dunamis in the Greek, Acts 1:8) or energy of divine grace. (Bullinger 1967, 257).

The dead in Christ will rise first or be resurrected first. Resurrection is a special act of divine grace carried out by the Holy Spirit. We who are alive and remain will be changed. How? By Holy Spirit, in a moment, in a twinkling of an eye, we will be changed and caught up in the air with Jesus. This is the catching away of the saints. All those people written in the Lamb's book of life are caught up in the air with Jesus. We do not know the day and we do not know the hour. But just like in the days of Noah, when the door on the ark shut, God shut it. The rain had started, the flooding had started. Now they are banging on the door of the Arc, but no one could open it. The Christians are gone, houses and cars are empty. Seats at school and in the theater are suddenly empty. Planes are crashing because the pilots are gone, and the cockpit is locked. The "Church Age" is over and the catching away for those written in the Lamb's book of life has occurred. It is too late for those left behind for this way into heaven.

---

[20] Notwithstanding in this rejoice not, that the spirits are subject unto you; but rather rejoice, because your names are written in heaven.

[21] In that hour Jesus rejoiced in spirit, and said, I thank thee, O Father, Lord of heaven and earth, that thou hast hid these things from the wise and prudent, and hast revealed them unto babes: even so, Father; for so it seemed good in thy sight.

—Luke 10:20-21 (KJV)

And I intreat thee also, true yokefellow, help those women which labored with me in the

> gospel, with Clement also, and with other my fellow laborers, whose names are in the book of life.
>
> —Philippians 4:3 (KJV)

> He that overcometh, the same shall be clothed in white raiment; and I will not blot out his name out of the book of life, but I will confess his name before my Father, and before his angels.
>
> —Revelation 3:5 (KJV)

> And there shall in no wise enter into it any thing that defileth, neither whatsoever worketh abomination, or maketh a lie: but they which are written in the Lamb's book of life.
>
> —Revelation 21:27 (KJV)

Now let us go back to the scripture 1 Corinthians 15:51. The second number mentioned is for the verse, 51. It is the same numbers as 15 just reversed. What does that mean? The number 51 is the number of divine revelation. So, you know God is going to reveal something to us when we read the scripture.

> Behold, I shew you a mystery; We shall not all sleep, but we shall all be changed,
>
> —1 Corinthians 15:51 (KJV)

This is just an example of the power in the Word of God. Verses 52 and 53 go on to explain the secret.

> ^{52} In a moment, in the twinkling of an eye, at the last trump: for the trumpet shall sound, and the dead shall be raised incorruptible, and we shall be changed.
>
> ^{53} For this corruptible must put on incorruption, and this mortal must put on immortality.
>
> —1 Corinthians 15:52-53 (KJV)

1 Thessalonians 4:17, goes on to explain that we who are alive and remain will meet the dead in Christ in the clouds and we will be with the Lord forever into eternity.

> ^{17} Then we which are alive and remain shall be caught up together with them in the clouds, to meet the Lord in the air: and so shall we ever be with the Lord.
>
> ^{18} Wherefore comfort one another with these words.
>
> —1 Thessalonians 4:17-18 (KJV)

The people who are left on earth will go through the Tribulation. It will be seven years long. We do not know the day it will begin. But we do know how long it will be. God does not want you to go through the Tribulation with the unbelievers. He wants your trust and belief in His only begotten Son Jesus as your personal Lord and Savior and to know that He, the Father, is "the only true God."

> [2] As thou hast given him power over all flesh, that he should give eternal life to as many as thou hast given him.
>
> [3] And this is life eternal, that they might know thee the only true God, and Jesus Christ, whom thou hast sent.
>
> —John 17:2-3 (KJV)

CHAPTER 3

The Tribulation Introduction

> And He shall confirm the covenant with many for one week: and in the midst of the week He shall cause the sacrifice and the oblation to cease, and for the overspreading of abominations he shall make it desolate, even until the consummation, and that determined shall be poured upon the desolate.
>
> —Daniel 9:27 (KJV)

The Tribulation Is Seven Years Long

The "catching away of the saints" (the "Rapture") has occurred. This ushers in the 1st year of the 7-year Tribulation. Daniels one week is really a week of years, or 7 years. This means the 5th dispensation is over when the dead in Christ rise and those that are alive and remain are caught up to meet the Lord in the air.

FIVE DISPENSATIONS HAVE PASSED

1. Adam brought in the dispensation of Innocence.

2. Noah brought in the dispensation of Human Government.

3. Abraham brought in the dispensation of The Promise (that the Lord was with him).

4. Moses brought in the dispensation of The Law.

5. Jesus brought in the dispensation of Grace and the Church age began in Acts 2.

Grace is now gone. Mercy is gone. Love, joy, peace, and longsuffering are all gone because now Holy Spirit and the fruit of the Spirit given to the saints of God, has been taken out of the way.

Ω

Holy Spirit, the Restrainer, Is Taken Out of the Way

The church, all born-again Christians that have accepted Jesus as Lord and Savior have Holy Spirit living in them. When the saints meet Jesus in the air, Holy Spirit is taken out of the way.

> 6 And now ye know what withholdeth that he might be revealed in his time.
> 7 For the mystery of iniquity doth already work: only he who now letteth will let, until he be taken out of the way.
> —2 Thessalonians 2:6-7 (KJV)

When Holy Spirit is taken out of the way (2 Thessalonians 2:7), He will no longer restrain sin, lawlessness or the antichrist and the antichrist inspired rebellion of all things God. This is much worse than the time of the falling away.

> [1] Now we beseech you, brethren, by the coming of our Lord Jesus Christ, and by our gathering together unto him,
>
> [2] That ye be not soon shaken in mind, or be troubled, neither by spirit, nor by word, nor by letter as from us, as that the day of Christ is at hand.
>
> [3] Let no man deceive you by any means: for that day shall not come, except there come a falling away first, and that man of sin be revealed, the son of perdition.
>
> —2 Thessalonians 2:1-3 (KJV)

> [1] Now the Spirit speaketh expressly, that in the latter times some shall depart from the faith, giving heed to seducing spirits, and doctrines of devils;
>
> [2] Speaking lies in hypocrisy; having their conscience seared with a hot iron.
>
> —1 Timothy 4:1-2 (KJV)

When the tribulation begins there will be a lawlessness that can only be described as chaos. People will allow themselves to be overtaken by seducing evil spirits and doctrines that are really developed by devils not God. There will be complete ridicule made of everything you find in the Bible. Now, "the son of perdition," "the man of sin" is about to arrive on the scene. To think that everything will be this much worse in the Tribulation is more than is imaginable. There will be an increase in evil activity to a level that has never been seen. Yet, God still wants to save the people He loves, and God still wants them to be a part of the Kingdom of God. The question is do they want God?

Ω

People Will Be Saved in the Tribulation

If you are reading this and have found yourself left behind in the Tribulation, know that God still loves you and wants to save you. Thank God you will still be able to be saved in the Tribulation. People from all over the world will be saved. It will be harder though, because of all the sin and violence on the earth. But know that God still loves you. He has allowed Holy Spirit to stay on the earth to help convict people of their sins and to help convert them to accept Jesus as Lord and Savior. Holy Spirit is successful, and it can be seen in Revelation 7:9-14.

> [9] After this I beheld, and, lo, a great multitude, which no man could number, of all nations, and kindreds, and people, and tongues, stood before the throne, and before the Lamb, clothed with white robes, and palms in their hands;

People will be saved in the Tribulation from every continent, every race, every creed, and every color. Some of those people will be martyrs. It will be hard. But just stand strong and have faith in God. It is not over until God says it is over. Do not fear because the Kingdom of God will last forever.

> And in the days of these kings shall the God of heaven set up a kingdom, which shall never be destroyed: and the kingdom shall not be left to other people, but it shall break in pieces and consume all these kingdoms, and it shall stand for ever.
>
> —Daniel 2:44 (KJV)

At the end of the Tribulation Jesus will return and establish the Kingdom of God on earth and it will last for 1,000 years and after that, into eternity. "It shall stand forever." "And the government shall be upon His shoulder," Isaiah 9:6. Your assignment will be to never renounce God.

Accept Jesus as Lord and Savior. Never take the mark of the beast. Stay strong.

Now let us walk through the main events of the Tribulation and do it in-a-snap.

Ω

Just a note: The war of Gog and Magog found in Ezekiel 38 will occur at some point, possibly after the catching away of the saints. No scholars can exactly pinpoint it. What we do know is that all the armies that will come to attack Israel will be caused by God to turn on each other, and they will be defeated.

CHAPTER 4

The Tribulation Begins: The First Six Seals Are Released

> Little children, it is the last time: and as ye have heard that antichrist shall come, even now are there many antichrists; whereby we know that it is the last time.
>
> —1 John 2:18 (KJV)

John is in Heaven. Who could be found that was worthy to open the book from the right hand of the Father? John wept because no one could be found.

Then Jesus, the Word, the Lamb of God, steps forward. He takes the book from the Father. The Lamb is the only person found worthy to open the book to do the Father's will and release the seven seals. All of heaven rejoices! Glory to God! (Revelation Chapter 5).

IN HEAVEN

This marks the beginning of the events in heaven after the catching away of the saints.

> And I saw when the Lamb opened one of the seals, and I heard, as it were the noise of thunder, one of the four beasts saying, Come and see.
>
> —Revelation 6:1

The beasts in heaven are given to help John understand everything that is happening.

> And I saw, and behold a white horse: and he that sat on him had a bow; and a crown was given unto him: and he went forth conquering, and to conquer.
>
> —Revelation 6:2 (KJV)

The person on the white horse here is the antichrist. He is coming and is placed in a position of power in the already started one world government to establish his peace plan on earth, but his real purpose is to conquer. His master, Satan, wants to be God and be worshipped like God. Putting the antichrist in position to rule and reign over the entire earth, albeit through satanic power, is Satan's first act. He will deceive those in charge of the one world government and all other governments that still exist.

ON EARTH

With all the missing people that were caught up in the air with Jesus, the turmoil trying to figure out where they are, if they are coming back, people being replaced in jobs that must function for the safety and care of all (like Air Traffic Controllers, Pilots, Doctors, Teachers, Military Officers, the Presidents of countries, Border security and many more). The minds of the people are consumed with all of that. Little notice is being paid to the changes in the spiritual world, the new "norm" which will affect them greatly.

The backdrop on earth is now the increase in evil activity and satanic power. Behind the scenes evil power will prevail. Where truth and justice once prevailed, now they will find that lies and deception rule the day. Yesterday, love and peace ruled the lives of many, now hate and fear prevail. Many who knew of God but had no relationship with God through His Son Jesus Christ will abandon even the weak beliefs that they had.

---

[10] And with all deceivableness of unrighteousness in them that perish; because they received not the love of the truth, that they might be saved.

[11] And for this cause God shall send them strong delusion, that they should believe a lie:

Even in the Tribulation you should follow the Word of God. The truth is that Jesus is our Lord and Savior, and "none can come unto the Father," Jesus says, "but by me." The Word of God is the absolute truth. It is your mirror into the mind of God and what He wants for you. But those that lie, and love lies, that believe that Jesus is not Lord and Savior, according to Revelation 22:15, will not go to be with Jesus in Heaven.

No one at this time will recognize who the antichrist really is. But there will be clues found in the Word of God.

HOW CAN YOU KNOW WHO
THE ANTICHRIST IS?

Little children, it is the last time: and as ye have heard that antichrist shall come, even now are there many antichrists; whereby we know that it is the last time.

—1 John 2:18

22 Who is a liar but he that denieth that Jesus is the Christ? He is antichrist, that denieth the Father and the Son.

23 Whosoever denieth the Son, the same hath not the Father: (but) he that acknowledgeth the Son hath the Father also.

—1 John 2:22

For many deceivers are entered into the world, who confess not that Jesus Christ is come in the flesh. This is a deceiver and an antichrist.

—2 John 1:7 (KJV)

So, the spirit of antichrist existed from when these scriptures were first written even to today. The information that there are now many antichrists, or people with the spirit of antichrist, tells us that we are in the last days or end of time (1John 2:18). 1 John 2:22-23 and 2 John 1:7 explains who the Bible considers the antichrist: he that denies that Jesus is the Christ, he that denies the Father and the Son, whoever denies the Son, and many deceivers who do not confess that Jesus Christ has come in the flesh.

Those left behind after the Rapture will not know who the antichrist is until the beginning of the last 3 ½ years of the Tribulation, but Daniel 9:27 gives us clues from the beginning.

> And he shall confirm the covenant with many for one week: and in the midst of the week he shall cause the sacrifice and the oblation to cease, and for the overspreading of abominations he shall make it desolate, even until the consummation, and that determined shall be poured upon the desolate.
>
> —Daniel 9:27 (KJV)

Daniel 9:27, And he shall confirm the covenant with many for one week: one week (of years) here is seven years. The person that confirms *(or in the Greek, strengthens)* the peace agreement or covenant is the antichrist. He will be the hero of the times. Because of him all sides will stay in the agreement. It is the strength of his word that makes everyone believe the peace agreement will work for them. No one could ever get peace in the Middle East to hold for any great length of time, but all signing parties will believe he can. This is also a sign of the beginning of the last seven years of human government.

The Temple in Jerusalem will be rebuilt, and they will be allowed to have animal sacrifices again. This may be part of the peace agreement. But in the middle of the seven years (in 3 ½ years) he makes them stop. We will discuss this part later in the book as already mentioned.

> ²³ And in the latter time of their kingdom, when the transgressors are come to the full, a king of fierce countenance, and understanding dark sentences, shall stand up.
>
> ²⁴ And his power shall be mighty, but not by his own power: and he shall destroy wonderfully, and shall prosper, and practice and shall destroy the mighty and the holy people.
>
> ²⁵ And through his policy also he shall cause craft to prosper in his hand; and he shall magnify himself in his heart, and by peace shall destroy many: he shall also stand up against the Prince of princes; but he shall be broken without hand.
>
> —Daniel 8:23-25 (KJV)

The antichrist will be fierce, *"but not by his own power"* but with satanic power. This power will make him stronger than anyone in the world. He will be able to take over or conquer the already existing one world government. The Word says the peace treaty is coming *"and by peace* (the antichrist) *shall destroy many."* The antichrist is coming after the saints have been caught up in the air, after the Rapture. There will be people left behind preaching messages offering salvation without repentance, without accepting Jesus as Lord and Savior. Do not believe them. Repent of your sin. Accept

Jesus as Lord and Savior. No one will get to the Father in Heaven "but by me," Jesus says.

> Jesus saith unto him, I am the way, the truth, and the life: no man cometh unto the Father, but by me.
>
> —John 14:6 (KJV)

Ω

The Second Seal Is Opened: The Red Horse

IN HEAVEN

> ³ And when he had opened the second seal, I heard the second beast say, 'Come and see.'
>
> ⁴ And there went out another horse that was red: and power was given to him that sat thereon to take peace from the earth, and that they should kill one another: and there was given unto him a great sword.
>
> —Revelation 6:3-4 (KJV)

The rider of the red horse was given power to take peace from the earth. The red horse is blood red signifying the blood of all the people that will be killing one another. Who could have peace with people dying all around you?

There will be war, murder, and violent death. People will kill one another at the drop of a hat for small things or any reason. No one can imagine just how bad this will be. No patience will be present on the earth. There will be no justice or innocent until proven guilty. Anyone that does not conform to the world as it exists will be killed. Anyone that has faith in Jesus as their Lord and Savior will be looked for to kill. Still, turn to God he will ultimately save you. You are a spirit being, you live in a body and you possess a soul, which is your mind, will and emotions.

Even if your body dies, your spirit will live on. Your soul goes where your spirit goes. With Jesus Christ as your Lord and Savior when your body dies, your spirit will live on in Heaven for eternity. If Jesus is not your Lord and Savior your spirit will live on in hell, separated from God for eternity (note: death is separation from God, so in hell is really death). Choose now who you will serve.

Ω

The Third Seal Is Opened: The Black Horse

IN HEAVEN

⁵ And when he had opened the third seal, I heard the third beast say, 'Come and see.' And I beheld, and lo a black horse; and he that sat on him had a pair of balances in his hand.

> [6] And I heard a voice in the midst of the four beasts say, A measure of wheat for a penny, and three measures of barley for a penny; and see thou hurt not the oil and the wine.
>
> —Revelation 6:5 (KJV)

ON EARTH

At this point famine will rule the day. Only the oil which represents the olive tree and the wine which represents the grapevine will not be affected. The famine will be worldwide and the prices for everything will be extremely high. The food will be scarce. With all the killing, war torn cities, and starvation, the black horse brings a dismal view, a feeling of being destitute of the light, a world filled with darkness. It is more than a feeling because the light of the world is gone at this point. The opposite of light, darkness prevails. The prince of darkness, the god of this world, Satan prevails. Everyone is experiencing existence on earth without the Holy Spirit intervening in the lives of men. Without the Holy Spirit bringing the "light of life" where God's people were protected from evil, because Holy Spirit lived in them.

> Then spake Jesus again unto them, saying, I am the light of the world: he that followeth me shall not walk in darkness, but shall have the light of life.
>
> —John 8:12 (KJV)

Holy Spirit is not living in people at this point. He has been taken out of the way. Life on earth is much harder at this point and it is going to get worse. Still, I urge you to trust that God will be there to get you to heaven if you will put your faith in Jesus even now.

Ω

The Fourth Seal Is Opened: The Pale Horse

IN HEAVEN

> [7] And when he had opened the fourth seal, I heard the voice of the fourth beast say, 'Come and see.'
>
> [8] And I looked and behold a pale horse: and his name that sat on him was Death, and hell followed with him. And power was given unto them over the fourth part of the earth, to kill with sword, and with hunger, and with death, and with the beasts of the earth.
>
> —Revelation 6:7-8 (KJV)

The pale horse and its rider represent an intensification of the deaths by hunger and disease. The wars will intensify, and more people will be killed by the sword or today by guns, tanks, bombs dropped by planes, released by submarines and ships, killed by animals of the earth and more. All this will be so severe to the point that a fourth of all people will die. Notice that hell followed with the pale horse rider.

Anyone that dies without being born again into the family of God by accepting Jesus as Lord and Savior is destined for hell. But it is not too late to accept Jesus as Lord and Savior. Look at the Fifth seal.

Ω

The Fifth Seal Is Opened: Martyr's Revealed

IN HEAVEN

> [9] And when he had opened the fifth seal, I saw under the altar the souls of them that were slain for the word of God, and for the testimony which they held:
>
> [10] And they cried with a loud voice, saying, 'How long, O Lord, holy and true, dost thou not judge and avenge our blood on them that dwell on the earth?'
>
> [11] And white robes were given unto every one of them; and it was said unto them, that they should rest yet for a little season, until their fellow servants also and their brethren, that should be killed as they were, should be fulfilled.
>
> —Revelation 6:9-11 (KJV)

The souls of the Martyred are crying out in heaven. They want to be avenged for all they went through. They are instructed to be patient. Many more people will be killed during the Tribulation. They are instructed to rest for a "little season until their fellow servants and their brethren, that should be killed as they were, should be fulfilled."

ON EARTH

People will look at all that is happening and realize that something is wrong. Where there was good now there is evil. There is no safety net. People will try to go off the grid, move to more rural areas where they feel safe and can grow their food. People will band together to possibly find safety in numbers. Many that knew about God but never accepted Jesus will begin to feel a witness deep in their soul. Many people will cry out, "What must I do to be saved?"

When they accept Jesus as Lord and Savior, if they are found out, they will be killed and become a Martyr. Is there something that the people should not do? Yes. They must not deny that Jesus is Lord. They must not accept the mark of the beast in their hand or forehead, and they must not worship the antichrist or his image. And when you think nothing could get worse, the sixth seal is released.

The Sixth Seal Is Released:
A Great Earthquake and Cosmic Judgements

IN HEAVEN

[12] And I beheld when he had opened the sixth seal, and, lo, there was a great earthquake;

and the sun became black as sackcloth of hair, and the moon became as blood;

13 And the stars of heaven fell unto the earth, even as a fig tree casteth her untimely figs, when she is shaken of a mighty wind.

14 And the heaven departed as a scroll when it is rolled together; and every mountain and island were moved out of their places.

15 And the kings of the earth, and the great men, and the rich men, and the chief captains, and the mighty men, and every bondman, and every free man, hid themselves in the dens and in the rocks of the mountains;

16 And said to the mountains and rocks, Fall on us, and hide us from the face of him that sitteth on the throne, and from the wrath of the Lamb:

17 For the great day of his wrath is come; and who shall be able to stand?

—Revelation 6:12-17 (KJV)

ON EARTH

The sixth seal released will first cause a "great earthquake." On April 18, 1906 when San Francisco experienced the "Great Earthquake" registering about 7.9, it propelled earthquake research and launched the first government-commissioned investigation into earthquakes called the US Geological Survey (USGS) –Earthquake Hazards Program. They had no money to fund the research, but the Carnegie Institution of Washington provided the funding. A landmark theory was developed "the theory of elastic rebound." This theory "forms the basis for our modern understanding of earthquakes." It "describes how the earth's crust gradually and elastically distorts with accumulating plate motion until it is suddenly returned to its undistorted state by rapid slip along a fault, releasing the years of accumulated strain and, in the process, generating seismic waves that produce shaking." (U.S. Geological Survey - Earthquake Hazards Program n.d.)

There will come a day when the sixth seal is released that the seismographs measurement will be blown out of the water. Instead of the tectonic plates moving back into their position, as described in the "theory of elastic rebound," according to the Word of God in Revelation 6:14 they will not move back. But every mountain and island will be in another position.

> And the heaven departed as a scroll when it is rolled together; and every mountain and island were moved out of their places.
> —Reveleation 6:14

If that is not enough, the Word says that stars will fall to earth. The word star in the Greek is the word aster. Close to our word asteroid. The word asteroid according to Vocabulary.com is, "any numerous small celestial bodies composed of rock and metal that move around the sun between the orbits of Mars and Jupiter. (Vocabulary.com n.d.)

An asteroid or meteoroid that hits the earth is a meteorite. In 2013, an asteroid made atmospheric entry and exploded over the Russian city Chelyabinsk and was "brighter than the sun."

> The explosion carried 20 to 30 times the energy of the Hiroshima atomic bomb.
>
> It was at that time estimated to be the largest known natural object to have entered Earth's atmosphere. It hit the earth as multiple meteorites. The shock wave blew windows in after a flash of light. Most of the injuries were from flying glass. Thousands of buildings were damaged in six cities across the region by the explosion's shock wave.
>
> —Byrd 2019

With all this in mind, the sixth seal releases stars from heaven, with an "s." The stress of life on earth with all this going on will become unbearable. There is no place to run and no place to hide.

> [15] And the kings of the earth, and the great men, and the rich men, and the chief captains, and the mighty men, and every bondman, and every free man, hid themselves in the dens and in the rocks of the mountains;
>
> [16] And said to the mountains and rocks, fall on us, and hide us from the face of him

that sitteth on the throne, and from the wrath
of the Lamb:

—Revelation 6:15-16

Everyone is afraid. There are seven types of people list-
ed Revelation 6:15. All seven types of people from the high-
est high in class structure to the lowest low in class structure
will seek refuge in the mountains. Everyone will be afraid.
The kings should call out to the King of kings and accept
Him as King, as Lord and as Savior. No one is greater than
the Great I Am. God wants us to care for the true riches,
getting souls saved, people born again. The riches of this
earth Jesus call mammon. You cannot serve God and earthly riches.

No man can serve two masters: for either he
will hate the one and love the other; or else he
will hold to the one, and despise the other. Ye
cannot serve God and mammon.

—Matthew 6:24 (KJV)

Again, the kingdom of heaven is like unto
treasure hid in a field; the which when a man
hath found, he hideth, and for joy thereof
goeth and selleth all that he hath, and buyeth
that field.

—Matthew 13:44 (KJV)

The Kingdom of God is the true treasure, the true riches can be found there. All the children of God must look forward to going home to the Kingdom of God which is the Kingdom of Heaven. Trust God. Pray to God. In the tribulation at this point, you must understand that neither your money nor your might will save you. Your status on the earth, great or small, will not save you. Instead of speaking to the mountains, speak to God the maker of heaven and earth and the mountains. Confess your sins. Accept Jesus and Lord and Savior. If you do that you will find His love not His wrath. Revelation 6:17 asks, "Who will be able to stand?" The children of God will stand. It is not too late even at this point in the Tribulation. It is extremely hard, but it is not too late. No matter what they do to you or promise to do to you. Depend on God. Trust God.

CHAPTER 5

The Witnesses

> ³ Saying, 'Hurt not the earth, neither the sea, nor the trees, till we have sealed the servants of our God in their foreheads.'
>
> ⁴ And I heard the number of them which were sealed: and there were sealed an hundred and forty and four thousand of all the tribes of the children of Israel.
>
> —Revelation 7:3-4 (KJV)

> ³ And I will give power unto my two witnesses, and they shall prophesy a thousand two hundred and threescore days, clothed in sackcloth.
>
> ⁴ These are the two olive trees, and the two candlesticks standing before the God of the earth.
>
> —Revelation 11:3-4 (KJV)

Who will tell the people left behind the truth about God and His Son Jesus? Will the God of Heaven really let the Prince of Darkness be left alone to wreak total havoc upon the world and its remaining people? The answer is a resounding no.

Before these witnesses came many men. Men filled with the Holy Spirit, inspired by God to write the Old Testament, or touched by Jesus, God the Son, in the New Testament. People were also moved by the Holy Spirit in the New Testament, although this time He was living in them. He was their teacher, their guide, their comforter, and their inspiration for writing the New Testament or New Covenant. The New Testament, the written will of God is sealed in the blood of our Lord and Savior Jesus Christ, the only begotten Son of our Father, the living God.

One such witness met Jesus on the road to Damascus. While he, Saul of Tarsus, was on that road to gather Christians and bring them back to Jerusalem for punishment, Saul came upon a bright blinding light. No one else traveling with Saul saw it. But when asked He identified Himself as Jesus. After that encounter Saul's name was changed to Paul. He became a powerful witness and the author of over two-thirds of the New Testament.

One of Paul's writings can be found in 2 Timothy 4:1-8:

> I charge thee therefore before God, and the Lord Jesus Christ, who shall judge the quick and the dead at His appearing and His kingdom;
>
> —2 Timothy 4:1

These are final instructions to Timothy from Paul. It is also a prophecy about the coming judgements for those living unsaved at the end of the Tribulation and those who have died unsaved. There will also be a judgment of the saved at the Judgement Seat of Christ after the catching away of the saints (or Rapture) while in heaven. This judgement is known as the "Bema" and will be discussed later.

> Preach the word; be instant in season, out of season; reprove, rebuke, exhort with all long-suffering and doctrine.
> —2 Timothy 4:2

The Word of God is the will of God. The Word is infallible. It is absolute truth. The Word of God is the final authority on every subject. The witness needs to be ready to say what is revealed to him (or her, today), "be instant" whether the person receives or rejects the information, whether they feel that the timing appears right or wrong, do what the Spirit reveals. The response should be "in season or out of season" as the Spirit leads. The response should teach what is right or what doctrine is. The response should teach what is not right, reprove or correct as a part of instruction.

> [3] For the time will come when they will not endure sound doctrine; but after their own lusts shall they heap to themselves teachers, having itching ears;
> [4] And they shall turn away their ears from the truth and shall be turned unto fables.
> —2 Timothy 4:3-4

This is a prophesy of the falling away that will also come at the end of time.

> But watch thou in all things, endure afflictions, do the work of an evangelist, make full proof of thy ministry.
>
> —2 Timothy 4:5

Do not give up come what may. Remain faithful to your calling in Christ Jesus.

> For I am now ready to be offered, and the time of my departure is at hand.
>
> —2 Timothy 4:6

Paul says he is now ready. We are human so we must be ready at the beginning when things start. Do not fret over small beginnings or large beginnings, each situation brings problems. We must be ready in the middle when the battle is raging and we are not sure by looking, at what the outcome will be. We must be ready at the end, when maybe we want to keep going but we are following God's timing. It is interesting the words "to be offered," not taken out by an attack of the enemy but offered as a sacrifice. The timing of the departure is in God's hands not ours.

> I have fought a good fight, I have finished my course, I have kept the faith:
>
> —2 Timothy 4:7

Verse 7 is a description at the heart of God found in every true witness of God. He fought a good fight. There will be a fight. The good fight of faith in God is the only good fight. "I have finished my course." Your course (not someone else's) is set for you by God in your mother's womb. (Jeremiah 1:4-5) The course that you follow to the best of your ability led by Holy Spirit your guide. (John 14:16-17) The witness wants to finish their course, not be stopped, not turn back, and not be prevented by the enemy, no matter how hard the fight is. And after all is said and done, the witness themselves want to say, "I have kept the faith." Those words give insight as to just how hard the fight is sometimes. "I have finished my course." Nothing is left on the table. The assignment God gave me is complete.

> Henceforth there is laid up for me a crown of righteousness, which the Lord, the righteous judge, shall give me at that day: and not to me only, but unto all them also that love his appearing.
>
> —2 Timothy 4:8 (KJV)

The dead in Christ shall rise first and then those that are alive and remain will be caught up in the air and go to heaven. In heaven everyone saved will go before Christ the righteous judge at the "Bema." Then the saved will receive a crown. It is called the crown of life according to James 1:12 and the crown of glory according to 1 Peter 5:4.

Just like God sent John the Baptist to be a witness to prepare the way of the Lord. The Lord's birth had been prophesied for thousands of years by the prophets. But, immediately prior to Jesus's arrival, John is found preaching repentance and the coming of someone greater than he was. By the time Jesus arrived, people were expecting Him. On the day John baptized Jesus, John was a witness of both Jesus and the Holy Spirt coming from heaven that day. God the Father was a witness of His Son that day as well. When Jesus came up out of the water Holy Spirit came upon Him in the form of a dove.

> [30] This is he of whom I said, 'After me cometh a man which is preferred before me: for he was before me.'
>
> [31] And I knew him not: but that he should be made manifest to Israel, therefore am I come baptizing with water.
>
> [32] And John bare record, saying, 'I saw the Spirit descending from heaven like a dove, and it abode upon Him.'
>
> [33] And I knew Him not: but He that sent me to baptize with water, the same said unto me, 'Upon whom thou shalt see the Spirit descending, and remaining on him, the same is he which baptizeth with the Holy Ghost.'
>
> [34] And I saw, and bare record that this is the Son of God.
>
> —John 1:30-34 (KJV)

And the Father introduced Jesus at the time of His baptism, again recorded in the book of Luke for all who paid attention.

> 21 Now when all the people were baptized, it came to pass, that Jesus also being baptized, and praying, the heaven was opened,
>
> 22 And the Holy Ghost descended in a bodily shape like a dove upon him, and a voice came from heaven, which said, Thou art my beloved Son; in thee I am well pleased.
>
> —Luke 3:21-22 (KJV)

So just like Jesus was introduced for His first coming, Jesus will be introduced for His second coming. Even though all the Christians who witnessed for over 2,000 years are gone, there will be witnesses to prepare the way, to set the stage for the most dramatic entry of all time. But that is not the only purpose of the preparation. The purpose is that God loves everyone in the world. He does not want anyone to perish. And as much as people may have heard the gospel before and dismissed the witness and the Word, God is getting ready to get everyone's attention.

Not to hurt anyone, but that everyone will come forward, recognize their sin, and ask, "What must I do to be saved?" People will know for sure who God is. There will be no question of His existence, power, and authority. Every knee at some point, this time, will bow. Every tongue at some point will this time declare that Jesus is Lord. See, God does not wish for any human to go through the Tribulation. But if you are in the Tribulation, know that God wants you to still end up in Heaven with Him. That is the reason God is sending the 144,000 witnesses.

Ω

144,000 Witnesses

Last time Jesus came as the Lamb of God. This time when He returns, He is coming as the Lion of the Tribe of Judah. The 144,000 witnesses are sealed by God in the first three and one-half years of the Tribulation. There will be 12,000 from each of the 12 tribes of the children of Israel. All will be male virgins. Their job is to witness to as many people as possible. What will they witness? They will witness the gospel, that the Kingdom of God is at hand. They will witness of Jesus, the Son of God, and His soon return. They will teach about Jesus being Lord and Savior and how it is not too late to accept Jesus. They, the witnesses themselves, will ultimately be in Heaven. They will teach, "do not let us go without you." "Be prepared to be one of the great multitudes from all nations that will stand before the throne of the Lamb in heaven. It will be hard but just believe."

> After this I beheld, and, lo, a great multitude, which no man could number, of all nations, and kindreds, and people, and tongues, stood before the throne, and before the Lamb,

Monoseta Burwell

clothed with white robes, and palms in their hands;

—Revelation 7:9 (KJV)

Palms in their hands reference that include the Jewish remnant (remember Palm Sunday).

At the same time there will be many false prophets teaching another gospel. But the scriptures warn you. Bibles will be scarce. I have at least ten on my bookshelf, so immediately after the catching away of the saints find Bibles and informational books like this one before the antichrist has them all confiscated.

[1] Beloved, believe not every spirit, but try the spirits whether they are of God: because many false prophets are gone out into the world.

[2] Hereby know ye the Spirit of God: Every spirit that confesseth that Jesus Christ is come in the flesh is of God:

[3] And every spirit that confesseth not that Jesus Christ is come in the flesh is not of God: and this is that spirit of antichrist, whereof ye have heard that it should come; and even now already is it in the world.

[4] Ye are of God, little children, and have overcome them: because greater is he that is in you, than he that is in the world.

—1 John 4:1-4 (KJV)

> ⁵ And now I beseech thee, lady, not as though I wrote a new commandment unto thee, but that which we had from the beginning, that we love one another.
>
> ⁶ And this is love, that we walk after his commandments. This is the commandment, That, as ye have heard from the beginning, ye should walk in it.
>
> ⁷ For many deceivers are entered into the world, who confess not that Jesus Christ is come in the flesh. This is a deceiver and an antichrist.
>
> —2 John 1:5-7 (KJV)

There will be many false reports saying that Jesus, the Messiah, never came the first time. This is deception, and deception is the opposite of truth. The Word of God, the Bible is the absolute truth, believe God. The reason that everything is dark is because the Kingdom of Satan is at work. Light is from God and the Kingdom of God and when Jesus left the first time, He left the Christians as the Light of the world. When they are "caught up" to be with Jesus, no more light will be present.

Jesus said something else about the Word of God. It looks like just words but the Word in the Bible is a living Word. It is your mirror to see yourself the way God sees you. As you read the Word, God will reveal Himself to you and His desires for you. Jesus described the Word like this:

> It is the spirit that quickeneth; the flesh prof-
> iteth nothing: the words that I speak unto
> you, they are spirit, and they are life.
> —John 6:63 (KJV)

Just remember, when you accept Jesus as Lord and Savior you are born again into the family of God and God, in
the person of the Holy Spirit, is in you.

> Ye are of God, little children, and have over-
> come them: because greater is he that is in
> you, than he that is in the world.
> —1 John 4 (KJV)

Remember, *"greater is He* (Holy Spirit) *that is in you, than he*
(Satan) *that is in the world."* God loves you. God is with you.
God is the same yesterday, today, and forevermore. Hold on
to God's unchanging hand.

The Two Witnesses

The two witnesses are in the temple for a thousand two
hundred and threescore days. That is three and one-half
years or forty and two months. There are parts of the Jewish remnant that are set to rebuild the temple, where they
will have sacrifices and offerings once again, just like in the
days of old.

> [1] And there was given me a reed like unto a rod: and the angel stood, saying, Rise, and measure the temple of God, and the altar, and them that worship therein.
>
> [2] But the court which is without the temple leave out, and measure it not; for it is given unto the Gentiles: and the holy city shall they tread under foot forty and two months.
>
> —Revelation 11:1-2 (KJV)

The gentiles will be all over the city and the temple court, but not inside. Nothing will be able to stop the completion of the temple or the altar, and the two witnesses are going to make sure of it. The gentiles will have run of the city of Jerusalem and the temple court for "forty and two months" which is three and one-half years. The first three and one-half years.

> [3] And I will give power unto my two witnesses, and they shall prophesy a thousand two hundred and threescore days, clothed in sackcloth.
>
> [4] These are the two olive trees, and the two candlesticks standing before the God of the earth.
>
> —Revelation 11:3-4 (KJV)

The two witnesses are one Elijah, most theologians agree. The second of the two witness's identity theologians disagree. Enoch was the only other man that did not die. So many believe he is probably the other witness. The other group believes that he could be Moses. They base that belief on the power exhibited in Revelation 11:6.

They are two olive trees. Look at how they were described in Zechariah 4:14.

> ^{12} And I answered again, and said unto him, 'What be these two olive branches which through the two golden pipes empty the golden oil out of themselves? '
>
> ^{13} And he answered me and said, 'Knowest thou not what these be? And I said, No, my lord.'
>
> ^{14} Then said he, 'These are the two anointed ones, that stand by the Lord of the whole earth.'
>
> —Zechariah 4:12-14 (KJV)

The two witnesses are the "anointed ones that stand by the Lord," now sent to the earth. They are "symbols of light-bearers," like Christ and they bring that light to the earth to witness to the people the glory of God and His Son Jesus.

> ^{5} And if any man will hurt them, fire proceedeth out of their mouth, and devoureth their enemies: and if any man will hurt them, he must in this manner be killed.

> ⁶ These have power to shut heaven, that it rain not in the days of their prophecy: and have power over waters to turn them to blood, and to smite the earth with all plagues, as often as they will.
>
> —Revelation 11:5 (KJV)

The witnesses have power to turn water into blood as in Exodus 4:9 when Moses prophesied to Pharaoh and the water became blood.

The position of this chapter in the Bible some believe that the two witnesses appear in the second three and one-half years. But they have a responsibility to make sure that the temple gets rebuilt, and they have been given the power to accomplish just that.

> And when they shall have finished their testimony, the beast that ascendeth out of the bottomless pit shall make war against them, and shall overcome them, and kill them.
>
> —Revelation 11:7

When the two witnesses have finished their assignment, their course, their testimony is complete, then Satan sends the antichrist to kill them. Satan cannot harm anyone until the assignment by God, has been completed.

> And their dead bodies shall lie in the street of the great city, which spiritually is called

> Sodom and Egypt, where also our Lord was crucified.
>
> —Revelation 11:8 (KJV)

The two dead witnesses will be placed on display in Jerusalem. Note that it is Jerusalem in the natural but spiritually it is now Sodom because of all the moral decay found there. It is called Egypt because of all the worldliness, the concern for things of the world and still not the things of God.

> [9] And they of the people and kindreds and tongues and nations shall see their dead bodies three days and an half, and shall not suffer their dead bodies to be put in graves.
>
> [10] And they that dwell upon the earth shall rejoice over them, and make merry, and shall send gifts one to another; because these two prophets tormented them that dwelt on the earth (KJV).
>
> —Revelation 11:9-10 (KJV)

The people mentioned here were so happy that the two witnesses were dead they had many parties. They sent gifts to each other in celebration like it was Christmas. They believed their trouble was over. Remember they had had famines, asteroids, economic failure and more. But instead of repenting to God, asking for forgiveness, and turning to Jesus as their Lord and Savior, they are in rebellion. Rebellion is an evil spirit that they should not follow. But they find out they were wrong.

> ¹¹ And after three days and a half, the Spirit of life from God entered into them, and they stood upon their feet; and great fear fell upon them which saw them.
>
> ¹² And they heard a great voice from heaven saying unto them, Come up hither. And they ascended up to heaven in a cloud; and their enemies beheld them.
>
> —Revelation 11:11-12 (KJV)

Holy Spirit enters the two witness, they are given life, and they stand upright. Now the people who have been happy are now afraid. They hear "a great voice from heaven" calling the two witnesses home just like the voice in Revelation 4:1 calling John, "Come up hither." And they ascend into heaven in a cloud like Jesus did in Luke 24:50.

> And the same hour was there a great earthquake, and the tenth part of the city fell, and in the earthquake were slain of men seven thousand: and the remnant were affrighted and gave glory to the God of heaven.
>
> —Revelation 11:13

The remnant of those saved gave glory to God but were still afraid as they felt the earthquake and saw a tenth of

Jerusalem being destroyed by the earthquake. They were afraid also by the thousands, seven thousand to be exact died. I am sure they are remembering Psalms 91, verse 7: "A thousand shall fall at thy side, and ten thousand at thy right hand; but it shall not come nigh thee" (KJV).

---

[14] The second woe *(the earthquake)* is past; and behold, the third woe cometh quickly.

[15] And the seventh angel sounded; and there were great voices in heaven, saying, The kingdoms of this world are become the kingdoms of our Lord, and of his Christ; and he shall reign for ever and ever.

—Revelation 11:14-15 (KJV)

"And the seventh angel sounded his trumpet" . . . and the many voices from heaven spoke with a proclamation to the saved remnant and a warning to the unsaved. Great voices in heaven said in Revelation 11:15:

The kingdoms of this world are become the kingdoms of our Lord, and of his Christ; and he shall reign for ever and ever.

—Revelation 11:15 (KJV)

Amen!

CHAPTER 6

The Great Tribulation: Satan Assembles His Leadership!

> 15 When ye therefore shall see the abomination of desolation, spoken of by Daniel the prophet, stand in the holy place, (whoso readeth, let him understand:)
>
> 16 Then let them which be in Judaea flee into the mountains:
>
> 17 Let him which is on the housetop not come down to take anything out of his house:
>
> 18 Neither let him which is in the field return back to take his clothes.
>
> —Matthew 24:15-18 (KJV)

The purpose of someone who leads, according to Noah Webster's 1828 dictionary, is to guide by hand or conduct by showing the way. The person who leads has implied authority, like a general who leads his troops into battle.

But this leadership led by the antichrist has Satan as the true authority. The people who will ultimately be led into battle against the Lord would be best described as not led, but drawn, enticed, or even led astray. The Bible tells us that even the elect will be deceived. They will be led into error, or led the wrong way, and even led to their death and ultimately to their second death eternally (which will be discussed in a future chapter.)

Ω

The Abomination of Desolation

> [11] And from the time that the daily sacrifice shall be taken away, and the abomination that maketh desolate set up, there shall be a thousand two hundred and ninety days.
>
> [12] Blessed is he that waiteth, and cometh to the thousand three hundred and five and thirty days.
>
> [13] But go thou thy way till the end be: for thou shalt rest, and stand in thy lot at the end of the days.
>
> —Daniel 12:11-13 (KJV)

Until now there was no proof as to who the anti-Christ is. The two witnesses have made sure that the temple is rebuilt. They have been arrested, killed, laid dead in the street while everyone made merry, risen from the dead and ascended into heaven. There is no one left to stop the anti-Christ from doing what he is being led by Satan to do. That is to go into the temple and proclaim that he is god. That is the abomination of desolation described by the prophet Daniel.

Lucifer had long planned this day from the time he was in Heaven. He and two-thirds of the angels made war with God and was unsuccessful, cast out and down to earth.

---

[12] How art thou fallen from heaven, O Lucifer, son of the morning! how art thou cut down to the ground, which didst weaken the nations!

[13] For thou hast said in thine heart, I will ascend into heaven, I will exalt my throne above the stars of God: I will sit also upon the mount of the congregation, in the sides of the north:

[14] I will ascend above the heights of the clouds; I will be like the most High.

[15] Yet thou shalt be brought down to hell, to the sides of the pit.

—Isaiah 14:12-15 (KJV)

Now the antichrist is standing in the temple of God, proclaiming that he is God. To the Jews he is saying, "I am the Messiah." To the Muslims he is saying, "I am the Mahdi"; to the Buddhists he is saying, "I am the 5th Buddha"; and to the Christians he is saying, "I am Christ." He will say, "I am all of these; I am one God. Follow me." This will be the time that the Jews are instructed by Jesus to flee to the mountains. Everyone should go to the mountains.

> ¹⁶ Then let them which be in Judaea flee into the mountains:
>
> ¹⁷ Let him which is on the housetop not come down to take anything out of his house:
>
> ¹⁸ Neither let him which is in the field return back to take his clothes.
>
> —Matthew 24:16-18 (KJV)

This is the Great Tribulation. The antichrist cancels the peace treaty. He demands that all sacrificing by the Jews cease and desist.

> And to the woman were given two wings of a great eagle, that she might fly into the wilderness, into her place, where she is nourished for a time, and times, and half a time, from the face of the serpent.
>
> —Revelation 12:14

The woman here is Israel that will flee into the wilderness for the last 3 ½ years of the Great Tribulation. Could the two wings of a great eagle's be the United States of America helping Israel? The wings that were on the lion in the book of Daniel are no more on the lion in the one world government in the book of Revelation. The nation with eagle's wings is not following the antichrist. That nation is protecting the woman Israel in the mountains for the last 3 ½ years (time, times, and half a time).

> [15] And the serpent cast out of his mouth water as a flood after the woman, that he might cause her to be carried away of the flood.
>
> [16] And the earth helped the woman, and the earth opened her mouth, and swallowed up the flood which the dragon cast out of his mouth.
>
> —Revelation 12:15

Even though the woman has fled to the mountains to Petra which is in Jordan, the enemy (the dragon or serpent is Satan) will pursue her to destroy her. He will cause a flood to ensue, but God prevents it from hurting her (Isaiah 59:19).

> And the dragon was wroth with the woman and went to make war with the remnant of her seed, which keep the commandments of God, and have the testimony of Jesus Christ.
>
> —Revelation 12:17 (KJV)

Remember there will be many that have heard the witnesses, the 144,000 male witnesses and the two witnesses at the Temple. There will be many that have accepted Christ and are keeping the commandments of God instead of following the antichrist. These people will be severely persecuted.

> And I stood upon the sand of the sea, and saw a beast rise up out of the sea, having seven heads and ten horns, and upon his horns ten crowns, and upon his heads the name of blasphemy.
>
> —Revelation 13:1

This verse is filled with symbolism. The sand of the sea is where the "sand" is a multitude of unsaved people in the "sea" of the now "wicked nations." The beast here is the one world government that existed at the time of the rapture or catching away of the saints but now the anti-Christ has taken over. "Seven" is the number of perfection good or evil and there are seven evil heads. The "head" is a symbol of intelligence and rulership. These seven heads represent world empires that existed in the past as defined empires such as Egypt, Assyria, Babylon, Medo-Persia, Greece, Rome, and the antichrists revived Roman Empire. These seven heads had ten horns where "ten" is the number meaning "order, testing and trial." The seven rulers have seven "horns", "a symbol of power, strength, and defense," will fall in lockstep order behind the antichrist where they will be tested and tried. On the ten horns are ten "crowns" representing kingship (Conner 1992).

Now they are kings in the kingdom of darkness where the antichrist now is ruling on earth. But God says in the Word that upon his heads is "the name of blasphemy." This whole government is against God, it speaks against God, blaspheming His Name, claims kingship in the Kingdom of Darkness and worships the antichrist and therefore Satan instead of God.

> And the beast which I saw was like unto a leopard, and his feet were as the feet of a bear, and his mouth as the mouth of a lion: and the dragon gave him his power, and his seat, and great authority.
>
> —Revelation 13:2

The one world government, at that point, has now evolved into one well-oiled machine given power and great authority by Satan, which is all evil. Germany the leopard, Russia the bear, and his mouth the mouth of a lion is England. The spokesperson for the government is the antichrist, which Satan has given him his seat as head of it all, with all the power and authority of hell itself.

The Anti-Christ Is Killed and Healed

> And I saw one of his heads as it were wounded to death; and his deadly wound was healed: and all the world wondered after the beast.
>
> —Revelation 13:3

Jesus died and was resurrected by the power of the Holy Spirit. The antichrist, who has proclaimed that he is god, seemingly demonstrates that power. After he is supposedly killed from a deadly wound, he is then healed by Satanic power. "And the (entire) world wondered (or intensely went, in the Greek) after the beast" who has demonstrated (or deceived them into believing) that he is god. Because in their mind only a god could do such a thing, but the devil can also through satanic power and does.

> And they worshipped the dragon which gave power unto the beast: and they worshipped the beast, saying, 'Who is like unto the beast? who is able to make war with him?'
> —Revelation 13:4

The people will be deceived and begin to believe that the antichrist is able to win against God who is sending all the attacks against the people of the earth. If he can come back to life from the dead, they are thinking no one can beat him. They are thinking if he is killed again, he will just come back to life. Then Satan gives him even more power.

> And there was given unto him a mouth speaking great things and blasphemies; and power was given unto him to continue forty and two months.
> —Revelation 13:5

Now he has the momentum, the people believe, and he has the power to continue for "forty and two months," or the last 3 ½ years of human government.

> ⁶ And he *(the antichrist)* opened his mouth in blasphemy against God, to blaspheme his name, and his tabernacle, and them that dwell in heaven.
>
> ⁷ And it was given unto him *(by satanic power)* to make war with the saints, and to overcome them: and power was given him over all kindreds, and tongues, and nations.
>
> ⁸ And all that dwell upon the earth shall worship him, whose names are not written in the book of life of the Lamb slain from the foundation of the world.
>
> —Revelation 13:6-8 (KJV)

Those that are saved, refuse to take the mark of the beast in the Great Tribulation, and will not worship him, will suffer great persecution. Remember that God does everything from the end to the beginning.

> ⁹ Remember the former things of old: for I am God, and there is none else; I am God, and there is none like me,
>
> ¹⁰ Declaring the end from the beginning, and from ancient times the things that are not

> yet done, saying, My counsel shall stand, and
> I will do all my pleasure.
>
> —Isaiah 46:9-10 (KJV)

The enemy will not win this end-time war. God will win and it is already done. Before this end time where now in Revelation 13:6 the antichrist has power and the control of the government, before he persecutes those whose names are written in the Lambs book, the end-time war has been won. Before this next group has accepted Jesus as Lord and Savior after the catching away of the saints; before all the remaining people worship the antichrist, remember that Jesus was slain before the foundation of the world and this war has already been won.

> [9] If any man have an ear, let him hear.
> [10] He that leadeth into captivity shall go into captivity: he that killeth with the sword must be killed with the sword. Here is the patience and the faith of the saints.
>
> Revelation 13:9-10 (KJV)

Through it all, the saints must have faith in God and patience to believe in the Word of God. They will witness so much death and destruction but must keep their faith in Jesus as Lord and Savior, keep the commandments of God, and keep their allegiance to Jesus Christ.

The False Prophet

The false prophet is the head of the one world religion, Apostate Christianity, where the antichrist has proclaimed that he is god. The false prophet's job is to direct the people to have faith in and worship the antichrist as god.

> [11] And I beheld another beast *(the false prophet)* coming up out of the earth; and he had two horns like a lamb, and he spake as a dragon.
> [12] And he exerciseth all the power of the first beast before him, and causeth the earth and them which dwell therein to worship the first beast, whose deadly wound was healed.
> —Revelation 13:11-12

The false prophet looks like a lamb of the one true God, but when he speaks, he gives himself away because he speaks with a voice identical to Satan the dragon. He will deny Jesus as Lord and Savior and he will blaspheme God. But remember 1 John 2:22-23.

> [22] Who is a liar but he that denieth that Jesus is the Christ? He is antichrist, that denieth the Father and the Son.

> ²³ Whosoever denieth the Son, the same hath not the Father: (but) he that acknowledgeth the Son hath the Father also.
>
> —1 John 2:22-23 (KJV)

He will cause the people of the earth to worship the anti-Christ because of the satanic magic he can perform.

> ¹³ And he doeth great wonders, so that he maketh fire come down from heaven on the earth in the sight of men,
>
> ¹⁴ And deceiveth them that dwell on the earth by the means of those miracles which he had power to do in the sight of the beast; saying to them that dwell on the earth, that they should make an image to the beast, which had the wound by a sword, and did live.
>
> ¹⁵ And he had power to give life unto the image of the beast, that the image of the beast should both speak, and cause that as many as would not worship the image of the beast should be killed.
>
> —Revelation 13:13-15 (KJV)

The false prophet tells them to *"make an image to the beast, which had the wound by a sword, and did live."* Then just like right out of a Star Wars movie he gives life to the image, possibly even like a hologram, and demands that if the people do not worship this image of the antichrist they will be killed.

The Mark of the Beast

So how will they know whether the people worship the image or the antichrist himself? The dragon, the antichrist, or the false prophet will never depend on the people to tell the truth because the whole Kingdom of Darkness is built on lies. They will have to have the mark of the beast, the number 666 as a chip, a branding, a tattoo, or some other method, to be in their right hand or in their forehead.

> [16] And he causeth all, both small and great, rich and poor, free and bond, to receive a mark in their right hand, or in their foreheads:
>
> [17] And that no man might buy or sell, save he that had the mark, or the name of the beast, or the number of his name.
>
> [18] Here is wisdom. Let him that hath understanding count the number of the beast: for it is the number of a man; and his number is Six hundred threescore and six.
>
> —Revelation 13:16-18 (KJV)

So, everyone, no matter what class, or walk of life will be slaves to the Kingdom of Darkness with no way to get out of it. You will not be able to buy anything, not even food to eat. You will not be able to have a business to sell anything for money not even food.

This mark is the number of man, the number six 3 times. What does the number mean? The first number is the number 6, the number of man, who is imperfect without God. The 66 or second six is the number of "pride and absolute dominion." The number three is the number of God and divine perfection. But the number 666 is the "pride of satanic guidance" or man who makes himself god, like the antichrist (Johnston 1990).

This mark will prevent you from getting to the true and living God and into the Kingdom of Heaven. The mark is the profession of faith in Satan. Do not take the mark or chip or whatever it is. The false prophet will make it seem very benign, like it does not mean anything in the beginning. But there is no free-will here on earth in this one world government.

Everyone who refuses to receive the mark will be persecuted and many will be killed. Those martyred will automatically be ushered into the Kingdom of Heaven. God never wanted anyone to go through the Tribulation or the Great Tribulation. That is why He sent His only begotten Son Jesus, our Savior. Accept Him now, do not wait. No one knows the day or the hour of your last breath on earth or the beginning of the Tribulation. You definitely do not want to wait until the Great Tribulation, these last 3 ½ years.

The leadership is complete. The method to bring in the rest of the people of the world is complete. But God steps in and we see the witnesses and all the people from every race creed and culture that are saved out of the Great Tribulation, now in heaven.

Monoseta Burwell

> ^{1} And I looked, and, lo, a Lamb stood on the mount Sion, and with him an hundred forty and four thousand, having his Father's name written in their foreheads.
>
> ^{2} And I heard a voice from heaven, as the voice of many waters, and as the voice of a great thunder: and I heard the voice of harpers harping with their harps:
>
> ^{3} And they sung as it were a new song before the throne, and before the four beasts, and the elders: and no man could learn that song but the hundred and forty and four thousand, which were redeemed from the earth.
>
> —Revelation 14:1-3 (KJV)

The two witnesses are in heaven and now the 144,000 and all that were saved from their witness of Jesus as Lord and Savior, are in heaven. Who is left to witness to the rest of the people on earth? Does God now give up on those who are left? The answer is a resounding no. God is still longsuffering at this point, still being unwilling to abandon those who have abandoned Him. At this point, but not forever, God still sends witnesses. This time they are angels.

> ^{6} And I saw another angel fly in the midst of heaven, having the everlasting gospel to preach unto them that dwell on the earth, and to every nation, and kindred, and tongue, and people,

⁷ Saying with a loud voice, Fear God, and give glory to him; for the hour of his judgment is come: and worship him that made heaven, and earth, and the sea, and the fountains of waters.

—Revelation 14:6-7 (KJV)

CHAPTER 7

The Great Tribulation: The Seventh Seal Brings Silence In Heaven!

> [22] And except those days should be shortened, there should no flesh be saved: but for the elect's sake those days shall be shortened.
>
> [23] Then if any man shall say unto you, Lo, here is Christ, or there; believe it not.
>
> [24] For there shall arise false Christs, and false prophets, and shall shew great signs and wonders; insomuch that, if it were possible, they shall deceive the very elect.
>
> —Matthew 24:22-24 (KJV)

All the earth is still filled with people at enmity with God. Yes, they have experienced what they think is the wrath of God during the first three and one-half years of the Tribulation. Many have turned to God now to accept Him. But even more believe they could deal with those blows from God and question, "Is that all God has?" They have decided that the antichrist with all the power of hell itself, will win this coming war. Satan has an idea of what he is up against but the followers of the antichrist on earth have no idea that they are going to lose. Even as the world thinks about the wars in the past, this time they believe they are sitting on the right side of history. They believe they are following someone that has the power, even supernatural power that will bring the dead back to life. Maybe some wrongfully believe that even they could be brought back to life if they are killed.

This time even the elect will be deceived. The church, Jesus's elect, has three and one-half years ago been caught up to meet Him in the air. The elect on earth now are the descendants of Abraham, Isaac, and Jacob, whose God parted the Red Sea and the river Jordan. The God that was a cloud by day and fire by night for the children of Israel, as they spent forty years being led by God through the wilderness. They were led by the one true and living God. It is their descendants now that will be deceived. This is the group that will not flee to the mountains as Jesus recommended in Matthew 24:16-18. There will be Jews that recognize that no man, no flesh could ever be God, except Jesus, the Messiah. The Jews that listen will be the ones who heard the sermon of the two witnesses or the 144,000 witnesses. Maybe they have been procrastinating, waiting to accept Jesus as Lord and Savior. But when they see the Abomination of Desolation standing where he should not, as described by Daniel and prophesied by the Witnesses, declaring that he is god, they that are listening and believe will flee to the mountains. Other Jews and Gentiles will not flee and will stay because they are deceived.

The deceived will go through the Great Tribulation and still be separated from God. They will have decisions to make. "Do I take the mark of the beast? Do I die by possible beheading, or turn from the beast, and listen to the angel witnesses who have come to take the place of all the other witnesses who are gone and in heaven?" They should turn from the beast and accept Jesus as Lord and Savior, which will allow them to be saved. Then try to escape by running to the mountains and pray they can get there.

One thing is true, God still loves them. He still wants to save them. Trust God.

The Seventh Seal

And when he had opened the seventh seal, there was silence in heaven about the space of half an hour.

—Revelation 8:1 (KJV)

As the abomination of desolation walks into the temple as foretold by prophets, men inspired by God, the seventh angel appears. Jesus is preparing to open the seventh of the seven seals that were discussed in Chapter four. The seventh seal opening brings silence as God the Father anticipates what is to happen next. No one in heaven is prepared for the response of God, to the insults, the hatred of all things heaven that only the once cherub of heaven would bring.

> ¹³ Thou hast been in Eden the garden of God; every precious stone was thy covering, the sardius, topaz, and the diamond, the beryl, the onyx, and the jasper, the sapphire, the emerald, and the carbuncle, and gold: the workmanship of thy tabrets and of thy pipes was prepared in thee in the day that thou wast created.
>
> ¹⁴ Thou art the anointed cherub that covereth; and I have set thee so: thou wast upon the holy mountain of God; thou hast walked up and down in the midst of the stones of fire.
>
> ¹⁵ Thou wast perfect in thy ways from the day that thou wast created, till iniquity was found in thee.
>
> ¹⁶ By the multitude of thy merchandise they have filled the midst of thee with violence, and thou hast sinned: therefore I will cast thee as profane out of the mountain of God: and I will destroy thee, O covering cherub, from the midst of the stones of fire.
>
> —Ezekiel 28:13-16 (KJV)

Satan does not send the antichrist to walk into the temple to worship God, once Lucifer's God too. No, Lucifer has become Satan, the devil, and this is his son the antichrist. The antichrist is just like his father, a liar and with all evil reigning supreme in the antichrist's soul. He has no love for the Father, the true and living God. The antichrist hates God like Satan hates God.

As the antichrist walks into the temple on earth, the seventh angel appears before the Father in heaven. For thirty minutes of silence. Could it be that the all loving, all knowing God, is on pause to give Satan one last chance to fall on his knees and say like the prodigal he is, "I want to come home. I'm sorry for all I have done against you." But no, the antichrist stands in the temple of God and proclaims that he is God. This antichrist is no Jesus Christ who was obedient to do the will of His Father. Jesus Christ who was sinless. Jesus Christ who was obedient to His Father even unto death.

Yes, heaven is silent because of what is coming. No holy, holy, holy, Lord God Almighty. No halleluiah. No praise the Lord. For thirty long minutes heaven is silent. It seems like eternity itself. God is not happy about what He is now compelled to do because He is a just God. None of the things happening in the Tribulation are designed for humans. John 3:16 says, "For God so loved the world that He gave His only begotten Son, that whosoever believeth in Him should not perish, but have everlasting life," in heaven with God. But this unsaved group is in the army of the antichrist, not the army of the Lord Jesus Christ.

The opening of the seventh seal by Jesus releases the seven angels who are given seven trumpets.

Ω

> And I saw the seven angels which stood before
> God; and to them were given seven trumpets.
> —Revelation 8:2

With each trumpet that the angels sound, the wrath of God will increase upon the earth. But before the first trumpet sounds another angel appears.

> ³ And another angel came and stood at the altar, having a golden censer; and there was given unto him much incense, that he should offer it with the prayers of all saints upon the golden altar which was before the throne.
> ⁴ And the smoke of the incense, which came with the prayers of the saints, ascended up before God out of the angel's hand.
> ⁵ And the angel took the censer, and filled it with fire of the altar, and cast it into the earth: and there were voices, and thunderings, and lightnings, and an earthquake.
> —Revelation 8:3-5 (KJV)

Before the seven trumpets begin to sound, God our Father takes time to listen to all the prayers of the saints found within the smoke of the incense. God answers prayers. Many are praying intercessory prayers for the lost still on earth. Many on earth have now seen more people leave and go to heaven thanks to the angel witnesses. Maybe they are now praying that they too could come to heaven after they accept Jesus at this late date, as Lord and Savior. He is the only way. God, the Father, who is loving, caring, merciful, and able to do above what anyone could ask or think, receives the prayers. And God answers the prayers in His divine providence before the first trumpet sounds.

The First Four Trumpets Sounds

> ^{6} And the seven angels which had the seven trumpets prepared themselves to sound.
>
> ^{7} The first angel sounded, and there followed hail and fire mingled with blood, and they were cast upon the earth: and the third part of trees was burnt up, and all green grass was burnt up.
>
> —Revelation 8:6-7

One third of the trees are burnt completely up and all the green grass. The smoke causes problems breathing but also the trees and the grass that are burnt up, are no longer able to take the carbon dioxide from the atmosphere and release oxygen. That will affect breathing.

> [8] And the second angel sounded, and as it were a great mountain burning with fire was cast into the sea: and the third part of the sea became blood;
>
> [9] And the third part of the creatures which were in the sea, and had life, died; and the third part of the ships were destroyed.
>
> —Revelation 8:8-9

Hawaii has the Mauna Loa volcano. It is considered the one of the largest volcanoes on earth. Could that be the great mountain cast into the sea? Hawaii is also in the "ring of fire" a horseshoe shaped area that surrounds the Pacific Ocean that contains many volcanoes. Only God knows the answer.

Just when people thought maybe they could escape by sea, even on a cruise ship, something happens. A third part of the creatures, fish and mammals that were in the sea and a third part of ships with all the people on them were destroyed so that a third part of the sea became blood. No sooner than all this happened then the third angel sounded.

> [10] And the third angel sounded, and there fell a great star from heaven, burning as it were a lamp, and it fell upon the third part of the rivers, and upon the fountains *(in the Greek, source)* of waters;
>
> [11] And the name of the star is called Wormwood: and the third part of the waters

Monoseta Burwell

became wormwood; and many men died of the waters, because they were made bitter.

—Revelation 8:10-11

A great star falls from heaven and must split apart to reach a third part of all the rivers and areas of fresh water. Many men will die from drinking the water because it will be bitter and poisonous. This is a fulfillment of the prophesy in Deuteronomy 29:18-21, fulfilled then and forever, holding true for Jews and Gentiles alike in the end-times. They must choose whom they will serve.

[18] Lest there should be among you man, or woman, or family, or tribe, whose heart turneth away this day from the LORD our God, to go and serve the gods of these nations; lest there should be among you a root that beareth gall and wormwood;

[19] And it come to pass, when he heareth the words of this curse, that he bless himself in his heart, saying, I shall have peace, though I walk in the imagination of mine heart, to add drunkenness to thirst:

[20] The LORD will not spare him, but then the anger of the LORD and his jealousy shall smoke against that man, and all the curses that are written in this book shall lie upon him, and the LORD shall blot out his name from under heaven.

> ²¹ And the LORD shall separate him unto
> evil out of all the tribes of Israel, according to
> all the curses of the covenant that are written
> in this book of the law.
> —Deuteronomy 29:18-21 (KJV)

No sooner than the people begin to die when one third of all the water of the rivers and fresh water becomes poisonous, the fourth angel sounded.

> And the fourth angel sounded, and the third
> part of the sun was smitten, and the third part
> of the moon, and the third part of the stars;
> so as the third part of them was darkened,
> and the day shone not for a third part of it,
> and the night likewise.
> —Revelation 8:12

Darkness or absence of light for one third of the day and night, what could this mean for earth's inhabitants? They will know there is a difference. Will they expect the antichrist to fix it? Before they have a chance to really evaluate the situation another angel flies through the midst of heaven explaining something worse to come. It is so bad that all the angel could say is, "Woe (in the Greek, grief), woe, woe, to the inhibiters of the earth" when the next three trumpets sound. Everyone has already experienced the worst imaginable. Why would they not turn to the true and living God to save them?

> And I beheld, and heard an angel flying
> through the midst of heaven, saying with a
> loud voice, Woe, woe, woe, to the inhabiters
> of the earth by reason of the other voices of
> the trumpet of the three angels, which are yet
> to sound!
>
> —Revelation 8:13 (KJV)

The Fifth Trumpet Sounds

The fifth angel sounds before the inhabitants on earth can really figure out what is going on.

> And the fifth angel sounded, and I saw a star
> fall from heaven unto the earth: and to him
> was given the key of the bottomless pit.
>
> —Revelation 9:1

A star falls from heaven to the earth and was given the key. This star is Lucifer that became Satan, that Jesus spoke of in Luke 10:18. To him was given "the key of the bottomless pit." Many times, Satan, the accuser of the brethren, has been allowed access to the throne of God since his original fall. Day and night, he accused the brethren before God, but no more (Job 1:9; Job 2:5; Zechariah 3:1; Revelation 12:10.) Now Satan has been given the key to the bottomless pit. He has a choice. Leave it closed and demonstrate his care for the people of the world. Try to convince them to follow God and not him, to avoid his fate. Or open the pit and torment the people for the five months that he has been allowed. He opens the bottomless pit. After this, Satan is not spoken of until he himself is put there for a thousand years by another angel (to be discussed later).

> ^{2} And he opened the bottomless pit; and there arose a smoke out of the pit, as the smoke of a great furnace; and the sun and the air were darkened by reason of the smoke of the pit.
> ^{3} And there came out of the smoke locusts upon the earth: and unto them was given power, as the scorpions of the earth have power.
>
> —Revelation 9:2-3

These are demonic locusts that have an assignment to hurt only the people that have not accepted Jesus as their Lord and Savior and do not have the seal of God in their foreheads.

> ^{4} And it was commanded them that they should not hurt the grass of the earth, neither any green thing, neither any tree; but only those men which have not the seal of God in their foreheads.
> ^{5} And to them it was given that they should not kill them, but that they should be tormented five months: and their torment

was as the torment of a scorpion, when he striketh a man.

⁶ And in those days shall men seek death and shall not find it; and shall desire to die, and death shall flee from them.

—Revelation 9:4-6

People will want to die because the pain is so great, so excruciating, but they will not die. These people are deceived to believe that this locust attack is caused by God. That is a lie. These are a Satanic attack of his demons. The locusts will persecute people on the earth for five months. They would persecute the people and kill the people except they are not allowed to. God only allows the locusts to be released and gives them guidelines of what they can and cannot do. The locusts cannot attack God's people, "neither any tree," "tree" being symbolic of the followers of God (Psalms 1:1-3; Matthew 7:15-20).

¹ Blessed is the man that walketh not in the counsel of the ungodly, nor standeth in the way of sinners, nor sitteth in the seat of the scornful.

² But his delight is in the law of the LORD; and in his law doth he meditate day and night.

³ And he shall be like a tree planted by the rivers of water, that bringeth forth his fruit in

his season; his leaf also shall not wither; and whatsoever he doeth shall prosper.

Psalms 1:1-3 (KJV)

---

[17] Even so every good tree bringeth forth good fruit; but a corrupt tree bringeth forth evil fruit.

[18] A good tree cannot bring forth evil fruit, neither can a corrupt tree bring forth good fruit.

[19] Every tree that bringeth not forth good fruit is hewn down and cast into the fire.

[20] Wherefore by their fruits ye shall know them.

—Matthew 7:17-20 (KJV)

This time they are stopped from destroying even Satan's own people. Satan does not love anyone. He wants to destroy all humans because he knows God loves them. That is true. God loves them and us. Repent. Accept Jesus as Lord and Savior and be saved.

---

[7] And the shapes of the locusts were like unto horses prepared unto battle; and on their heads were as it were crowns like gold, and their faces were as the faces of men.

[8] And they had hair as the hair of women, and their teeth were as the teeth of lions.

Monoseta Burwell

> ⁹ And they had breastplates, as it were breastplates of iron; and the sound of their wings was as the sound of chariots of many horses running to battle.
>
> ¹⁰ And they had tails like unto scorpions, and there were stings in their tails: and their power was to hurt men five months.
>
> ¹¹ And they had a king over them, which is the angel of the bottomless pit, whose name in the Hebrew tongue is Abaddon, but in the Greek tongue hath his name Apollyon.
>
> —Revelation 9:7-11

In the Greek, Apollyon means destroyer. There is one whose job description is described by Jesus and is a destroyer.

> The thief cometh not, but for to steal, and to kill, and to destroy.
>
> —John 10:10 (KJV)

He is the king over them, the fallen angel now called the prince of the Kingdom of Darkness, Satan himself. Satan's instruction to the locusts would be to kill his followers. But God says, no you can only hurt them for five months. Give them five months to come to the knowledge of the truth.

> One woe is past; and, behold, there come two
> woes more hereafter.
>
> —Revelation 9:12

Ω

The Sixth Trumpet Sounds

No sooner than those five months end the sixth angel sounds his trumpet in heaven and one more "woe" or grief causing event comes.

> [13] And the sixth angel sounded, and I heard a voice from the four horns of the golden altar which is before God,
>
> [14] Saying to the sixth angel which had the trumpet, Loose the four angels which are bound in the great river Euphrates.
>
> [15] And the four angels were loosed, which were prepared for an hour, and a day, and a month, and a year, for to slay the third part of men.
>
> —Revelation 9:13-15 (KJV)

The sixth angel released four angels who had been preparing for what is to come. They were preparing to kill "the third part of men" with 200 million demonic horsemen. This time the antichrists and Satan's followers will not just be injured, they will die. Repent now. Do not wait. Accept Jesus as Lord and Savior.

---

¹⁶ And the number of the army of the horsemen were two hundred thousand: and I heard the number of them.

¹⁷ And thus I saw the horses in the vision, and them that sat on them, having breastplates of fire, and of jacinth, and brimstone: and the heads of the horses were as the heads of lions; and out of their mouths issued fire and smoke and brimstone.

¹⁸ By these three was the third part of men killed, by the fire, and by the smoke, and by the brimstone, which issued out of their mouths.

¹⁹ For their power is in their mouth, and in their tails: for their tails were like unto serpents, and had heads, and with them they do hurt.

—Revelation 9:16-19 (KJV)

A third part of the people will be killed with the fire, smoke and brimstone which come out of the horse's mouth. These people who will be killed will go to hell. Other people will be injured by the tail of the demonic horse which was like a serpent. The people that are not killed will still not turn to God. They do not repent of their evil ways but continue to worship Satan, because of the deception of the antichrist and false prophet, which is real even today. They will love the sin life more than being saved. They will worship devils and idols made with hands that can "neither see, nor hear, nor walk:"

> And the rest of the men which were not killed by these plagues yet repented not of the works of their hands, that they should not worship devils, and idols of gold, and silver, and brass, and stone, and of wood: which neither can see, nor hear, nor walk:
>
> —Revelation 9:20

They did not repent of the sins that are the most prominent in the Tribulation.

> Neither repented they of their murders, nor of their sorceries, nor of their fornication, nor of their thefts.
>
> —Revelation 9:21 (KJV)

They did not repent of "their murders," there will be no consideration for life during the Tribulation. "Nor of their sorceries," the word sorcery in the Greek is "pharmekeia" which means drugs, that will put this current day drug use to shame. The occult will be prominent, including contacting the dead and witchcraft on a level never seen before with supernatural power from Satan himself. Fornication and immorality on all levels will be running rampant. Thefts and lawlessness with no regard for personal property will be prevalent. There will be a lot of empty apartments and houses after the catching away of the saints, when people are martyred and the 144,000 are called home at the beginning of the Great Tribulation. These dwelling places are locations where people will just take over and become squatters. Revelation 9:21 states that they will not repent of any of that, even with the most horrific judgements from God. The people just continue to disregard the witnessing angels telling them what will save them, which is to accept Jesus as Lord and Savior, repent of their sin, and be saved. That, of course, is exactly what needs to be done even today.

Ω

The Seven Thunders Speak

Before the seventh angel sounds, something happens:

> [1] And I saw another mighty angel come down from heaven, clothed with a cloud: and a rainbow was upon his head, and his face was as it were the sun, and his feet as pillars of fire:
>
> [2] And he had in his hand a little book open: and he set his right foot upon the sea, and his left foot on the earth,
>
> [3] And cried with a loud voice, as when a lion roareth: and when he had cried, seven thunders uttered their voices.
>
> [4] And when the seven thunders had uttered their voices, I was about to write: and

> I heard a voice from heaven saying unto me, seal up those things which the seven thunders uttered and write them not.
>
> —Revelation 10:1-4

There are things like what the seven thunders say, that will be unknown. John was not allowed to write them in the book of Revelation.

> ⁵ And the angel which I saw stand upon the sea and upon the earth lifted up his hand to heaven,
>
> ⁶ And sware by him that liveth for ever and ever, who created heaven, and the things that therein are, and the earth, and the things that therein are, and the sea, and the things which are therein, that there should be time *(or delay)* no longer:
>
> ⁷ But in the days of the voice of the seventh angel, when he shall begin to sound, the mystery of God should be finished, as he hath declared to his servants the prophets.
>
> —Revelation 10:5-7 (KJV)

When the seventh angel sounds there will be no longer a mystery of God. No longer will there be a mystery of the return of Jesus Christ, and the establishment of His Kingdom. But before this, let us step back in time on earth, to the beginning of the Great Tribulation. Where the antichrist through the power of Satan, has prepared his leadership and begins to prepare his religious system and his commercial system on earth. Because of all the deception and Satanic power, as these areas develop, they trust and believe in the antichrist even more. Let us step back in time on earth to watch as they are ready to follow his lead, as the antichrist appears to rise before his fall, even to the battle of Armageddon, the ultimate fall.

CHAPTER 8

The Great Babylon Has Risen!

19 As many as I love, I rebuke and chasten: be zealous therefore, and repent.

20 Behold, I stand at the door, and knock: if any man hear my voice, and open the door, I will come in to him, and will sup with him, and he with me.

21 To him that overcometh will I grant to sit with me in my throne, even as I also overcame, and am set down with my Father in his throne.

—Revelation 3:19-21 (KJV)

4 And the woman was arrayed in purple and scarlet color, and decked with gold and precious stones and pearls, having a golden cup in her hand full of abominations and filthiness of her fornication:

5 And upon her forehead was a name written, MYSTERY, BABYLON THE GREAT,

The enemy is deceptive and complex. He misleads the people causing them to make errors in their decisions. He causes them to believe the opposite of the truth, which are lies. Jesus said in John 8:32, ". . . *Know the truth and the truth shall make you free.*" The unsaved person who uses their intellect alone is no match for the enemy Satan. This is spiritual warfare. Only the person who has accepted Jesus as their Lord and Savior is given spiritual armor. This armor is the armor of God to protect the saved from all the attacks of the enemy. (Ephesians 6:11; 2 Corinthians 6:7) But even the saved must use the armor, and put it on daily, and preferably never take it off, for the protection to be effective. The enemy is attacking every person on all fronts. The unsuspecting, unsaved person is not even aware of the attack. Once the person is positioned for defeat, the enemy delivers the final blow. Death is the final blow, but not for the saved, because Jesus defeated hell, death, and the grave, the saved have been given life.

> O death, where is thy sting? O grave, where is thy victory?
> —1 Corinthians 15:55 (KJV)

> I am he that liveth, and was dead; and, be-
> hold, I am alive for evermore, Amen; and
> have the keys of hell and of death.
>
> —Revelation 1:18 (KJV)

Jesus came the first time so that we could have life and life more abundantly during our lifetime and now into eternity. Jesus has the keys to hell and death and we who are saved, therefore, have victory over death. So even though your body dies your spirit will live on. We are spirit beings; we live in a body and we possess a soul. Our soul is our mind, will and emotions. Our soul will go wherever our spirit goes. Death is separation from God when your body dies. Life is eternal with God when Jesus is your Lord and Savior when your body dies. Choose life.

Ω

Babylon the Great

In the book of Jeremiah, the prophet prophesied about the day when the true and living God would make a new covenant with all his people, written in their heart. First the New Testament or Covenant came to pass with the church, the followers of Christ and during the Tribulation, when the Jewish elect, the house of Israel, accepts the New Covenant.

^{31} Behold, the days come, saith the LORD, that I will make a new covenant with the house of Israel, and with the house of Judah:

^{32} Not according to the covenant that I made with their fathers in the day that I took them by the hand to bring them out of the land of Egypt; which my covenant they brake, although I was an husband unto them, saith the LORD:

^{33} But this shall be the covenant that I will make with the house of Israel; After those days, saith the LORD, I will put my law in their inward parts, and write it in their hearts; and will be their God, and they shall be my people.

^{34} And they shall teach no more every man his neighbor, and every man his brother, saying, Know the LORD: for they shall all know me, from the least of them unto the greatest of them, saith the LORD: for I will forgive their iniquity, and I will remember their sin no more.

^{35} Thus saith the LORD, which giveth the sun for a light by day, and the ordinances of the moon and of the stars for a light by night, which divideth the sea when the waves thereof roar; The LORD of hosts is his name.

—Jeremiah 31:31-35 (KJV)

And this prophesy in Jeremiah came true as all prophesies in the Old and New Testaments (or Covenants), inspired by God, written by men. There are other prophesies concerning the first Babylon and the end time Great Babylon destruction. God's Word does not return to Him void but accomplishes all that He says.

> Flee out of the midst of Babylon, and deliver every man his soul: be not cut off in her iniquity; for this is the time of the LORD'S vengeance; he will render unto her a recompence.
>
> —Jeremiah 51:6

It is now the Great Tribulation and nearing the day of the Lord's vengeance. This is a warning to leave this government of the antichrist. Do not listen to the world religion taught by the false prophet. Do not be cut off from God in the mix with the iniquity of this world government system under the authority of the antichrist and Satan. God is preparing to bring destruction to it all.

> 7 Babylon hath been a golden cup in the LORD'S hand, that made all the earth drunken: the nations have drunken of her wine; therefore the nations are mad.
>
> 8 Babylon is suddenly fallen and destroyed: howl for her; take balm for her pain, if so be she may be healed.

> [9] We would have healed Babylon, but she is not healed: forsake her, and let us go every one into his own country: for her judgment reacheth unto heaven, and is lifted up even to the skies.
>
> —Jeremiah 51:7-9 (KJV)

Babylon is a symbol of the one world system both religious and political which includes its commerce, which is all under Satan's control and wicked during the Tribulation. Religious Babylon with its one world religion and apostate Christianity is represented by the Great Whore, led by the false prophet. The Harlot, apostate Christianity, who is subject to and worships Satan instead of being subject to and worshipping God, tricks the nations and all worldly people to follow her. They have a form of godliness but deny the true power of God. The true power that leads the one world religion is Satan.

> [1] And there came one of the seven angels which had the seven vials, and talked with me, saying unto me, 'Come hither; I will shew unto thee the judgment of the great whore that sitteth upon many waters:'
>
> [2] With whom the kings of the earth have committed fornication, and the inhabitants of the earth have been made drunk with the wine of her fornication.
>
> [3] So he carried me away in the spirit into the wilderness: and I saw a woman sit upon

> a scarlet colored beast, full of names of blas-
> phemy, having seven heads and ten horns.
> —Revelation 17:1-3

This beast is the one world government or political Babylon which has names of blasphemy or speaking evil against
God. Political Babylon worships the antichrist.

> And the woman was arrayed in purple and
> scarlet color, and decked with gold and pre-
> cious stones and pearls, having a golden cup
> in her hand full of abominations and filthi-
> ness of her fornication:
> —Revelation 17:4

The woman, the Harlot, has a gold cup, beautiful and
enticing on the outside but filled on the inside with hatred
and iniquity that God calls abominations and filthiness.
The Harlot is focused on the antichrist, against God and
love for all things Satan.

> And upon her forehead was a name written,
> MYSTERY, BABYLON THE GREAT, THE
> MOTHER OF HARLOTS AND ABOMI-
> NATIONS OF THE EARTH.
> —Revelation 17:5 (KJV).

That scripture speaks to the Mystery of Babylon. It is
a mystery only because of deception. The people of the

world do not really understand what is going on but are mesmerized by the freedom to react to every variation of lust available like in Sodom. The people also love the things of this world system but have been instructed to come out from among the world and be separate from worldliness. They will not listen and will want to stay connected with the one world antichrist run government.

---

¹⁵ And what concord hath Christ with Belial? Or what part hath he that believeth with an infidel?

¹⁶ And what agreement hath the temple of God with idols? for ye are the temple of the living God; as God hath said, I will dwell in them, and walk in them; and I will be their God, and they shall be my people.

¹⁷ Wherefore come out from among them, and be ye separate, saith the Lord, and touch not the unclean thing; and I will receive you,

¹⁸ And will be a Father unto you, and ye shall be my sons and daughters, saith the Lord Almighty.

—2 Corinthians 6:15-18 (KJV)

Then as when this scripture in 2 Corinthians was written, sometime from 55-56 AD until now, God is telling us to come out and telling us that we cannot be a part of this type of Babylon world government, worshipping the beast and his image, and be a part of God. God says do not even touch the unclean thing, do not take the mark of the beast, and separate yourself unto Jesus Christ as Lord and Savior. Then God will be a Father to you and will accept you as one of His sons and daughters. You must escape to God. Wake up, you are being deceived. Repent of your sins and God is faithful and just to forgive you of your sin and to cleanse you of all unrighteousness (1 John 1:9, KJV).

This end-time one world government with the antichrist as the head, led by the power of Satan, will give their strength, political and military, to the antichrist.

> [14] These shall make war with the Lamb, and the Lamb shall overcome them: for he is Lord of lords, and King of kings: and they that are with him are called, and chosen, and faithful.
> [15] And he saith unto me, 'The waters which thou sawest, where the whore sitteth, are peoples, and multitudes, and nations, and tongues'.
> —Revelation 17:14-15 (KJV)

Many people are under the control of the nation's supporting the antichrist and his one world government. There will come a point where the influence of the false prophet will no longer be needed by the antichrist.

> And the ten horns which thou sawest upon the beast, these shall hate the whore, and shall make her desolate and naked, and shall eat her flesh, and burn her with fire.
> —Revelation 17:16

Any time you are dealing with the devil you are dispensable. In the middle of the Tribulation at the start of the Great Tribulation, the antichrist goes into the Temple and declares that he is god. At that point he demands that everyone worship him and that includes the false prophet. The false prophet who is the whore in Revelation 17:16, helps deceive everyone to take the mark of the beast. Who knows what happened between the two of them later, except we reach a point where most of the people have taken the mark of the beast? After that point, the antichrist and his one world political system, turn on the false prophet, to the point they begin to hate him and destroy his power. The antichrist is god overall, everything and every nation is under his control and he has the power of Satan leading him. How could anything go wrong? Or so he thinks.

> [17] For God hath put in their hearts to fulfil his will, and to agree, and give their kingdom unto the beast, until the words of God shall be fulfilled.
> [18] And the woman which thou sawest is that great city, which reigneth over the kings of the earth.
>
> —Revelation 17:17-18 (KJV)

Now the woman in this scripture is not the false prophet but more the spirit of Babylon that great city, which reigns over the kings. That spirit is the spirit of antichrist, Satan himself. The next time the false prophet is mentioned in scripture he is being thrown into the lake of fire. That will be discussed later.

> ²⁰ Behold, I stand at the door, and knock: if any man hear my voice, and open the door, I will come in to him, and will sup with him, and he with me.
>
> ²¹ To him that overcometh will I grant to sit with me in my throne, even as I also overcame, and am set down with my Father in his throne.
>
> ²² He that hath an ear, let him hear what the Spirit saith unto the churches.
>
> —Revelation 3:20-22 (KJV)

God is still at the door. Knock and the door will be opened. The door will be opened, and God will come into the people of the Great Babylon, and even to you. All you need to do is knock on God's door.

Most of the business leaders will not listen to that advice either. They have no idea of what is to come. They will not be prepared when it does. Why is that? They are listening to one side, the voice of the antichrist, and refuse to listen to the final witnesses, the angels.

CHAPTER 9

The Great Babylon Is Fallen

> [1] And after these things I saw another angel come down from heaven, having great power; and the earth was lightened with his glory.
>
> [2] And he cried mightily with a strong voice, saying, Babylon the great is fallen, is fallen, and is become the habitation of devils, and the hold of every foul spirit, and a cage of every unclean and hateful bird.
>
> [3] For all nations have drunk of the wine of the wrath of her fornication, and the kings of the earth have committed fornication with her, and the merchants of the earth are waxed rich through the abundance (or power) of her delicacies.
>
> —Revelation 18:1-3 (KJV)

This is now near the end of the Great Tribulation. All commerce is under the control of the antichrist and they are living it up. I am a retired Pastor but am still owner of my small business, so this part was especially interesting to me.

It appears the businesses have the world in the palm of their hands. They have more money than they could ever imagine. If the business owners want to survive in this one world government led by the antichrist, of course they must take the mark of the beast. They will not sell to anyone that does not have the mark of the beast. They will not employ anyone who does not have the mark of the beast. They cannot buy from any merchant that does not have the mark. These business owners are willing to sell their souls to the devil to stay in business. What a tragedy. But it is not new. It has been happening since the beginning of time. Instead of listening to the voice of Truth and following God, they are following what seems right to them.

> There is a way which seemeth right unto a man, but the end thereof are the ways of death.
> —Proverbs 14:12 (KJV)

> There is a way that seemeth right unto a man, but the end thereof are the ways of death.
> —Proverbs 16:25 (KJV)

Maybe the reason this was written two times in Proverbs by the wisest man that ever lived on the face of the earth, King Solomon, is because it is so easy to be deceived by what we think is right. We must realize with God you can be successful in your business. The Word of God explains how. There is a contrast between the godly (those who are obedient to the Word of God and separate themselves from the fellowship with the world) and the wicked. The wicked have fellowship with the world (in this case the one world government and the antichrist) and receive the counsel or advice from the world. When God gives counsel, it is to prevent us from being harmed not to prevent us from having fun or being successful. God knows the enemy wants to seduce us and deceive us so he can ultimately kill and destroy us.

> [1] Blessed is the man that walketh not in the counsel of the ungodly, nor standeth in the way of sinners, nor sitteth in the seat of the scornful.
>
> [2] But his delight is in the law of the LORD; and in his law doth he meditate day and night.
>
> —Psalms 1:1-2

The godly genuinely enjoys God and His Word and seeks to learn more and more every day. They want to understand and be obedient to God's Word out of the pleasure they receive from it.

> And he shall be like a tree planted by the rivers of water, that bringeth forth his fruit in his season; his leaf also shall not wither; and whatsoever he doeth shall prosper.
>
> —Psalms 1:3

It is now near the end of the Great Tribulation, and there is not much time left. But whatever time is left use it for God. God will be a source of protection for His people, He will guide you through until the end and you will live and prosper. Accept Jesus as Lord and Savior. You will not only live, but you will have life more abundantly, now and into eternity.

The ungodly will have a different end. They "shall perish."

> [4] The ungodly are not so: but are like the chaff which the wind driveth away.
>
> [5] Therefore the ungodly shall not stand in the judgment, nor sinners in the congregation of the righteous.
>
> [6] For the LORD knoweth the way of the righteous: but the way of the ungodly shall perish
>
> —Psalms 1:4-6 (KJV)

Everything is going to begin to unravel right before the antichrist and the one world government's eyes.

> And after these things *(everything that happened in chapter 17)* I saw another angel come down from heaven, having great power; and the earth was lightened with his glory.
>
> —Revelation 18:1

This is the angel from Revelation 14:8. This angel speaks prophetically of what is to immediately come to pass. This is nearing the very end of the Great Tribulation. All the nations under the control of the antichrist have believed the deception and taken part in all that he offered them.

> ² And he cried mightily with a strong voice, saying, Babylon the great is fallen, is fallen, and is become the habitation of devils, and the hold of every foul spirit, and a cage of every unclean and hateful bird.
>
> ³ For all nations have drunk of the wine of the wrath of her fornication, and the kings of the earth have committed fornication with her, and the merchants of the earth are waxed rich through the abundance *(power)* of her delicacies.
>
> ⁴ And I heard another voice from heaven, saying, Come out of her, my people, that ye be not partakers of her sins, and that ye receive not of her plagues.
>
> —Revelation 18:2-4 (KJV)

The Great Babylon is about to be destroyed but before the destruction comes, God sends another angel from heaven (this is the third angel from Revelation 14:8) to witness to anyone who will listen to come out from among those remaining in the Great Babylon. There are still some there who have not taken the mark of the beast but also have not made the decision to follow God. I wonder if some of them could even have been the merchants themselves.

> How much she hath glorified herself, and lived deliciously, so much torment and sorrow give her: for she saith in her heart, I sit a queen, and am no widow, and shall see no sorrow.
>
> —Revelation 18:7

The antichrist and his one world government stand in defiance to God and all the wrath of God that has gone on around them.

> [8] Therefore shall her plagues come in one day, death, and mourning, and famine; and she shall be utterly burned with fire: for strong is the Lord God who judgeth her.
>
> [9] And the kings of the earth, who have committed fornication and lived deliciously with her, shall bewail her, and lament for her, when they shall see the smoke of her burning,
>
> [10] Standing afar off for the fear of her torment, saying, Alas, alas, that great city Babylon, that mighty city! for in one hour is thy judgment come.
>
> [11] And the merchants of the earth shall weep and mourn over her; for no man buyeth their merchandise anymore.
>
> —Revelation 18:8-11 (KJV)

Monoseta Burwell

Babylon will be destroyed in one hour. The nations were deceived and stand "afar off" now afraid that they too will receive the same judgement. The merchants are upset, because they have no one to purchase their merchandise, not because their Babylon is destroyed, which is so predictable.

---

¹² The merchandise of gold, and silver, and precious stones, and of pearls, and fine linen, and purple, and silk, and scarlet, and all thyine wood, and all manner vessels of ivory, and all manner vessels of most precious wood, and of brass, and iron, and marble,

¹³ And cinnamon, and odors, and ointments, and frankincense, and wine, and oil, and fine flour, and wheat, and beasts, and sheep, and horses, and chariots, and slaves, and souls of men.

¹⁴ And the fruits that thy soul lusted after are departed from thee, and all things which were dainty and goodly are departed from thee, and thou shalt find them no more at all.

¹⁵ The merchants of these things, which were made rich by her, shall stand afar off for the fear of her torment, weeping and wailing,

—Revelation 18:12-15

The merchants will see what is happening to Babylon and they too "stand afar off" because they are afraid that they will be judged by God.

> ¹⁶ And saying, 'Alas, alas, that great city, that was clothed in fine linen, and purple, and scarlet, and decked with gold, and precious stones, and pearls!'
>
> ¹⁷ For in one hour so great riches is come to nought. And every shipmaster, and all the company in ships, and sailors, and as many as trade by sea, stood afar off,
>
> ¹⁸ And cried when they saw the smoke of her burning, saying, 'What city is like unto this great city!'
>
> ¹⁹ And they cast dust on their heads, and cried, weeping and wailing, saying, Alas, alas, that great city, wherein were made rich all that had ships in the sea by reason of her costliness! for in one hour is she made desolate.
>
> —Revelation 18:16-19 (KJV)

The shipmasters, sailors, and ship companies that traded by the sea "stood afar off," and cried their eyes out because Babylon has been destroyed in one hour. They were crying because their source of great riches had come to a sudden end.

> ²⁰ Rejoice over her, thou heaven, and ye holy apostles and prophets; for God hath avenged you on her.
>
> ²¹ And a mighty angel took up a stone like a great millstone, and cast it into the sea, say-

ing, 'Thus with violence shall that great city Babylon be thrown down, and shall be found no more at all.'

[22] And the voice of harpers, and musicians, and of pipers, and trumpeters, shall be heard no more at all in thee; and no craftsman, of whatsoever craft he be, shall be found any more in thee; and the sound of a millstone shall be heard no more at all in thee;

[23] And the light of a candle shall shine no more at all in thee; and the voice of the bridegroom and of the bride shall be heard no more at all in thee: for thy merchants were the great men of the earth; for by thy sorceries were all nations deceived.

—Revelation 18:20-23 (KJV)

Babylon the Great has fallen. All the nations, merchants, ships, and sailors were deceived along with all the musicians, craftsmen and others who listened to and followed the false prophet and the antichrist and their sorcery. None of the many warnings and teachings of the two witnesses, the 144,000 witnesses or the angel witnesses were heeded or followed by these people. Now the final judgement comes, "that great city Babylon" is thrown down and this time "she shall be found no more at all" Revelation 18:23.

> And in her was found the blood of prophets, and of saints, and of all that were slain upon the earth.
>
> —Revelation 18:24 (KJV)

The spirit of Babylon has been responsible for all the blood of the prophets, saints, and all the martyrs and others slain on the earth from the beginning of time. It was the spirit of antichrist, Satan himself.

The mystery is about to be opened for all to see and understand:

> And to make all men see what is the fellowship of the mystery, which from the beginning of the world hath been hid in God, who created all things by Jesus Christ.
>
> —Ephesians 3:9 (KJV)

Do not underestimate the power of God. He can still save you and your family. Listen to the angel in Revelation 18:1. He has just left the presence of God and you can see the glory of God all over him by the light. Jesus said:

> And I, if I be lifted up from the earth, will draw all men unto me.
>
> —John 12:32 (KJV)

The angel is lifting the Name of Jesus, the angel is speaking but Jesus is the One that is doing the drawing. It is Jesus that is tugging on your heart strings to follow Him. Trust Jesus as your Savior because He is, and He will lead you all the way to the end and into eternity.

CHAPTER 10

Before the Seventh Vial: Satan Prepares His Armies for Armageddon

> [6] And the seven angels came out of the temple, having the seven plagues, clothed in pure and white linen, and having their breasts girded with golden girdles.
>
> [7] And one of the four beasts *(that are in the midst of and around the throne of God)* gave unto the seven angels seven golden vials full of the wrath of God, who liveth for ever and ever.
>
> [8] And the temple was filled with smoke from the glory of God, and from his power; and no man was able to enter into the temple, till the seven plagues of the seven angels were fulfilled.
>
> —Revelation 15:6-8 (KJV)

The temple is filled with the smoke of the Presence of God; no one can enter. The time for repentance and salvation is over. No one can enter to intercede or persevere in prayer, to plead with God on behalf of another, not any longer. No one can call on the Name above every Name, the Name of Jesus and expect help, not any longer. It is now time for the enemies of God to feel the final wrath of God. No one can enter the presence of God again until "the seven plagues of the seven angels" are fulfilled.

> [1] And I heard a great voice out of the temple saying to the seven angels, 'Go your ways, and pour out the vials of the wrath of God upon the earth.'
>
> [2] And the first went and poured out his vial upon the earth; and there fell a noisome and grievous sore upon the men which had the mark of the beast, and upon them which worshipped his image.
>
> —Revelation 16:1-2

The only people spared from this were those still on the fence and had not accepted the mark of the beast, had not worshipped his image, but also had not yet accepted Jesus as Lord and Savior.

> [3] And the second angel poured out his vial upon the sea; and it became as the blood of a dead man: and every living soul died in the sea.
>
> [4] And the third angel poured out his vial upon the rivers and fountains of waters; and they became blood.
>
> —Revelation 16:3-4

No more ships can float in the water on the earth because it has become "as the blood of a dead man." The blood coagulates upon death becoming thick and clots until ultimately total blockage occurs. Everything living in the water of the earth after this, dies.

> [5] And I heard the angel of the waters say, 'Thou art righteous, O Lord, which art, and wast, and shalt be, because thou hast judged thus.'
>
> [6] For they have shed the blood of saints and prophets, and thou hast given them blood to drink; for they are worthy.
>
> [7] And I heard another out of the altar say, 'Even so, Lord God Almighty, true and righteous are thy judgments'.
>
> —Revelation 16:5-7 (KJV)

The wrath of God is being poured out now on the enemies of God who do not want to be saved but prefer to continue to remain with the antichrist, at enmity with God. God is holy and righteous and at this point is distributing punishment for all the evil on the earth and to all those who chose to follow evil. Those who refuse to repent but choose to follow the Kingdom of Darkness, the prince who is Satan himself, will receive the wrath of God.

> [6] Then shall I not be ashamed, when I have respect unto all thy commandments.

> [7] I will praise thee with uprightness of heart, when I shall have learned thy righteous judgments.
>
> —Psalms 119:6-7 (KJV)

It is our responsibility to respect the commandments of God our Father who created everything including us. It is our responsibility to learn the Truth as found in the Word of God. The Word is our mirror into what we should look like, found only in the heart of our Father, our creator.

> [8] And the fourth angel poured out his vial upon the sun; and power was given unto him to scorch men with fire.
>
> [9] And men were scorched with great heat, and blasphemed the name of God, which hath power over these plagues: and they repented not to give him glory.
>
> —Revelation 16:8-9

The heat is so hot that it burns mankind. Did they repent of their hatred and sin? No, they cursed God.

> [10] And the fifth angel poured out his vial upon the seat of the beast; and his kingdom was full of darkness; and they gnawed their tongues for pain,

> ¹¹ And blasphemed the God of heaven
> because of their pains and their sores and re-
> pented not of their deeds.
>
> —Revelation 16:10-11

The seat of Satan is now being affected; these are all his leadership and followers in authority. They are now becoming confused because their world is becoming darker and what they thought was a clear path forward with the antichrist, is in question. They now are afflicted with sores and great pain to the point of biting holes their tongues. Did this cause them to repent, turn from their wicked ways and choose to follow God? No. They hated God even more.

> And the sixth angel poured out his vial upon
> the great river Euphrates; and the water
> thereof was dried up, that the way of the
> kings of the east might be prepared.
>
> —Revelation 16:12

Just like in the past against the original Babylon the water is dried up (Jeremiah 50:38, KJV). This time it is so the kings of the east who have done God's bidding in the past will be used again. Ultimately Babylon will fall as it did in the past (Jeremiah 50:48, KJV).

> ¹³ And I saw three unclean spirits like frogs
> come out of the mouth of the dragon, and

> out of the mouth of the beast, and out of the mouth of the false prophet.
>
> ¹⁴ For they are the spirits of devils, working miracles, which go forth unto the kings of the earth and of the whole world, to gather them to the battle of that great day of God Almighty.
>
> ¹⁵ Behold, I come as a thief. Blessed is he that watcheth, and keepeth his garments, lest he walk naked, and they see his shame.
>
> —Revelation 16:13-15

The frogs, the spirits of devils, work miracles before the kings of the earth to continue to lead them into deception. The kings look at those miracles and believe that with all that power, surely the antichrist can defeat God. It is a lie, but the kings fall for it.

In Revelation 16:15, Jesus himself offers one of seven blessings or beatitudes offered in the book of Revelation for those of us who not only read, but listen to and obey, the instructions found therein. The other six are found in Revelation 1:3, 14:13, 19:9, 20:6, 22:7, and 22:14.

> Behold, I come as a thief. Blessed is he that watcheth, and keepeth his garments, lest he walk naked, and they see his shame.
>
> —Revelation 16:15 (KJV)

We are instructed to watch, and continually watch for the second coming of the Lord. We do not know the hour;

we do not know the day, but we are looking for the return of our Lord and Savior Jesus Christ. While waiting, we are to remain clothed with the righteousness of Christ. Not our own righteousness but we who are saved have the righteousness of Christ. We must keep ourselves clothed. Our body is what our spirit is clothed with, called a tabernacle.

> [1] For we know that if our earthly house of this tabernacle were dissolved, we have a building of God, a house not made with hands, eternal in the heavens.
> [2] For in this we groan, earnestly desiring to be clothed upon with our house which is from heaven.
> —2 Corinthians 5:1-2 (KJV)

We are spirit beings, we live in a body and we possess a soul which is our mind, will and emotions. When Jesus calls us to meet Him at the gathering together of the saints in the clouds (commonly known as the Rapture) and when Jesus comes back on the Day of the Lord, we do not want to be ashamed. We do not want to be found naked, without our spirit being saved and clothed with our house from heaven.

Jesus ends His blessing with a reminder in Revelation 16:15 that He is coming as a thief in the night so you must be ready. You must be saved or born again into God's family, with the Spirit of God living in you.

Of course, this means nothing to the masses following the antichrist and the false prophet because they have not listened to the Pastors, Apostles, Prophets, Evangelists or

Teachers while they were still on earth. They have not listened to the two witnesses, the 144,000 witnesses, or the angel witnesses. They have only listened to the antichrist.

Now they are angry. They are positioning their armies for their final fight. The infamous battle that almost everyone has heard about, the battle of Armageddon, and they are going to lose.

> And he gathered them together into a place called in the Hebrew tongue Armageddon.
> —Revelation 16:16

No one can save them now. The presence of God is in the temple and no one, nothing can enter, no incense with prayers, nothing. Nothing can happen until the seventh angel pours the seventh vial.

> [17] And the seventh angel poured out his vial into the air; and there came a great voice out of the temple of heaven, from the throne, saying, It is done.
> [18] And there were voices, and thunders, and lightnings; and there was a great earthquake, such as was not since men were upon the earth, so mighty an earthquake, and so great.
> —Revelation 16:17-18

The first time we read "voices, and thunders, and lightnings; and there was a great earthquake" in Revelation 8:5, it was after the seventh seal and there was silence in heaven for 30 minutes. The second time was after the seventh trumpet sounded in Revelation 11:15 where the "kingdoms of this world are become the kingdoms of our Lord, and of his Christ and He shall reign for ever and ever." Now in Revelation 16:17 we read after the seventh vial is poured, "It is done."

---

¹⁹ And the great city *(Babylon)* was divided into three parts, and the cities of the nations fell: and great Babylon came in remembrance before God, to give unto her the cup of the wine of the fierceness of his wrath.

²⁰ And every island fled away, and the mountains were not found.

²¹ And there fell upon men a great hail out of heaven, every stone about the weight of a talent: and men blasphemed God because of the plague of the hail; for the plague thereof was exceeding great.

—Revelation 16:19-21 (KJV)

Still defiant, they gather to battle. They gather all over the world, this is a world-wide battle.

---

³² Thus saith the LORD of hosts, Behold, evil shall go forth from nation to nation, and a

> great whirlwind shall be raised up from the coasts of the earth.
>
> [33] And the slain of the LORD shall be at that day from one end of the earth even unto the other end of the earth: they shall not be lamented, neither gathered, nor buried; they shall be dung upon the ground.
>
> —Jeremiah 25:32-33 (KJV)

Before Christ returns on the Day of the Lord, He takes out time to be with His bride, at the Marriage Supper of the Lamb. What a day of rejoicing it will be.

CHAPTER 11

Armageddon, the End: the War for the World

---

[12] How art thou fallen from heaven, O Lucifer, son of the morning! how art thou cut down to the ground, which didst weaken the nations!

[13] For thou hast said in thine heart, I will ascend into heaven, I will exalt my throne above the stars of God: I will sit also upon the mount of the congregation, in the sides of the north:

[14] I will ascend above the heights of the clouds; I will be like the most High.

[15] Yet thou shalt be brought down to hell, to the sides of the pit.

—Isaiah 14:12-15 (KJV)

It's a Love Story

The entire Bible is a love story. When in the beginning of time our heavenly Father spoke, and the Word created the world and all that is in it through the power of the Holy

Spirit. A world that was perfectly designed by the Father, with a beautiful garden called Eden, for His son and His daughter to inhabit. They were given dominion, to oversee and rule over everything. They were given six thousand years of time for human government under the theocracy of God, the creator, ruler and owner of the Kingdom of heaven and the earth. Adam and Eve were given the task to be fruitful and multiply. How exciting.

By the third chapter of Genesis, human government had been diverted by an act of sin, from the Kingdom of God to the Kingdom of Darkness. They could eat of every tree in the garden except one, the tree of the knowledge of good and evil. Eve was deceived by Satan to eat from that one tree and then she gave it to her husband Adam to eat. Satan had said that they would not die, but they did. Their spirit died immediately and their beautiful flesh bodies, a masterpiece, would also ultimately die. Why? Because somehow eating of that fruit caused a genetic alteration, a genetic mutation which made Satan, the prince of darkness, their god as well as their king. Because after that mutation, Adam and Eve were under the dominion of evil, the law of sin and death. So, sin had dominion over them. Sickness had dominion over them as well as poverty and because of it, Adam had to toil to make ends meet. Because they were the mother and father of us all we inherited that same mutation.

The first Adam failed, but will the last Adam fail? A resounding no, he will not.

> For God so loved the world, that he gave his only begotten Son, that whosoever believeth in him should not perish, but have everlasting life.
>
> —John 3:16 (KJV)

The world is going to perish but men and women in the world should not, if they accept, believe in, the gift of Jesus Christ as Lord and Savior.

> [20] But now is Christ risen from the dead and become the first fruits of them that slept.
> [21] For since by man came death, by man came also the resurrection of the dead.
> [22] For as in Adam all die, even so in Christ shall all be made alive.
>
> —1 Corinthians 15:20-22 (KJV)

Death came into the world when Adam sinned. This death according to God is different than we as humans today perceive. The sin was an act of treason when Adam delivered the dominion or rulership that was given to him from God over the world, to another Kingdom out of the jurisdiction of its creator God. So, no longer is the rule of the world the extension of the good, the love and the peace, found in the Kingdom of Heaven.

God had warned Adam in Genesis 2:17 that he would surely die if he ate from the tree of the knowledge of good and evil. Adam only knew good, because God is good. All

God's commandments are good and will prevent you from being hurt or injured. Death according to God is loss of his connection with Adam, or being separated from God, the source of life. God is also the source of everything you should need, want, and desire. He is the source of everything that is good. Death is independence and disconnection from God. Adam lost rulership of the Kingdom of the world on earth. Satan knew that would happen and that the Kingdom of Darkness would then rule the world (Monroe 2010). That was the way it all started, where Satan thought he could win a war against God, because of the first Adam. He was wrong in the beginning, he is wrong now, and he will be wrong in the end.

> And I will put enmity between thee and the woman, and between thy seed and her seed; it shall bruise thy head, and thou shalt bruise his heel.
>
> —Genesis 3:15

From this scripture you will notice that there will be offspring from Satan. The antichrist is one of those offspring. The woman's offspring is Jesus Christ, the seed of Abraham, Isaac, and Jacob down through 14 and 4 generations. Through Jesus, we receive our authority back. In the power of the tongue, we can speak the Word of God and life into every situation. Through Jesus we are no longer under the law of sin and death. We are under the law of the Spirit of Life through Christ Jesus when we repent of our sins and receive Jesus as Lord and Savior. Jesus Christ is the seed that will bruise the head of Satan in the end.

This is a love story and the Bridegroom, Jesus, is coming to get His Bride the church first. He will not stop there because God wants everyone to be saved and to come into the knowledge of the truth. There is one mediator between God and men and that is Jesus.

> [3] For this is good and acceptable in the sight of God our Saviour;
>
> [4] Who will have all men to be saved, and to come unto the knowledge of the truth.
>
> [5] For there is one God, and one mediator between God and men, the man Christ Jesus.
>
> —1 Timothy 2:3-5 (KJV)

The Lord has watched the devil torment us for thousands of years. We have been on a path as the human race with wars, rumors of wars, sickness, disease, pandemics, and every other evil thing. It is near the end, but we must be ready when Jesus comes for us. Jesus explains it in the Parable of the 10 Virgins.

> Then shall the kingdom of heaven be likened unto ten virgins, which took their lamps, and went forth to meet the bridegroom.
>
> —Matthew 25:1 (KJV)

Just as in the ancient Hebrew wedding, the bride to be, was betrothed to the bridegroom, and then he went away to prepare a place for her. This period of waiting lasted until the place was prepared, and the groom was ready. The groom's readiness was determined by his father. The groom did not know when he would return, only the groom's father knew. Just as Jesus stated that He did not know when He would return, only the Father knew. (Smith, Phillips and Sanna 2011)

Jesus explained what he was going to be doing for us while he was gone in John 14:2.

> [1] Let not your heart be troubled: ye believe in God, believe also in me.
> [2] In my Father's house are many mansions: if it were not so, I would have told you. I go to prepare a place for you.
> —John 14:1-2

Jesus, the bridegroom has gone to prepare a place for us, His Bride. He explains that he will return to get us.

> [3] And if I go and prepare a place for you, I will come again, and receive you unto myself; that where I am, there ye may be also.
> —John 14:3 (KJV)

He is preparing a place for us, but in prayer when two or three are gathered in His Name, there He is in the midst. Jesus is Emmanuel, God with us. He will never leave us or forsake us. And Jesus is coming for us. Even if you die and your spirit is in heaven, your body will rise, because the dead in Christ rise first and the saints are caught up to meet Jesus in the clouds (the Rapture):

> ¹⁵ For this we say unto you by the word of the Lord, that we which are alive and remain unto the coming of the Lord shall not prevent them which are asleep.
>
> ¹⁶ For the Lord himself shall descend from heaven with a shout, with the voice of the archangel, and with the trump of God: and the dead in Christ shall rise first:
>
> ¹⁷ Then we which are alive and remain shall be caught up together with them in the clouds, to meet the Lord in the air: and so shall we ever be with the Lord.
>
> ¹⁸ Wherefore comfort one another with these words.
>
> —1 Thessalonians 4:15-18 (KJV)

Then they are taken to heaven to be made ready for the Marriage Supper of the Lamb (Revelation 19: 7-8.)

> ⁵ And a voice came out of the throne, saying, 'Praise our God, all ye his servants, and ye that fear him, both small and great.'
>
> ⁶ And I heard as it were the voice of a great multitude, and as the voice of many wa-

ters, and as the voice of mighty thunderings, saying, Alleluia: for the Lord God omnipotent reigneth.

7 Let us be glad and rejoice and give honor to him: for the marriage of the Lamb is come, and his wife hath made herself ready.

8 And to her was granted that she should be arrayed in fine linen, clean and white: for the fine linen is the righteousness of saints.

9 And he saith unto me, 'Write, Blessed are they which are called unto the marriage supper of the Lamb.' And he saith unto me, 'These are the true sayings of God'.

—Revelation 19:5-9 (KJV)

Back to the Parable of the 10 Virgins and the Bridegroom:

2 And five of them were wise, and five were foolish.

3 They that were foolish took their lamps, and took no oil with them:

—Matthew 25:2-3

Half of the women (the foolish) were not prepared to meet the Bridegroom. The oil is a type of the Holy Spirit. When you are born again into the family of God, Holy Spirit comes to live in you. To be prepared for the Bridegroom you must be born again, regenerated, or "re-gened." The mutation, the alteration in our genes that occurred when Adam sinned is corrected and Holy Spirit is able to live in us, not just be on us, like in the Old Testament, for a specific task.

Jesus's return is going to be at a time that is unexpected and by this indication, at least half of the people will not be ready.

> But the wise took oil in their vessels with their lamps.
> —Matthew 25:4

The wise know the Lord; have accepted Him as their personal Lord and Savior and they have a relationship with Him. No matter when He returns, they should be prepared, watching, and waiting for their soon coming King. The wise has Jesus as the Lamp unto their feet to lead them, direct them, and guide them. Even though they do not know the day or the hour, they are "consecrated, set aside from the world, and faithfully await His return." (Smith, Phillips and Sanna 2011)

> While the bridegroom tarried, they all slumbered and slept.
> —Matthew 25:5

The wise and the foolish virgins slept. The Groom is away preparing for His Bride and just like the ancient Hebrew wedding, the Father will say when it is time to return to get her. The Bride should be focused on all that she needs to do while waiting on the Bridegroom, not focused on things of this ever changing, ever spiraling downward, both spiritually and morally, world. We must continually renew our mind with the Word of God. We are in the world as ambassadors from the Kingdom, but not of the world. We are of the Kingdom of God, where heaven is our home.

The catching away of the saints or the "Rapture" will be a surprise and come at an unexpected time for everyone. The Day of the Lord at the end of the Great Tribulation, the end of the last 3 ½ years of the Tribulation, will also come at an unexpected time. It too will be a surprise.

> But the end of all things is at hand: be ye therefore sober and watch unto prayer.
> —1 Peter 4:7 (KJV)

We all need to be sober or alert and watch for the return of Jesus.

> And at midnight there was a cry made, 'Behold, the bridegroom cometh; go ye out to meet him.'
> —Matthew 25:6

In the ancient Hebrew weddings, you always needed oil for the wick to provide the light because the Bridegroom always came at night, mostly at midnight. All the family and friends were out celebrating and blowing a shofar, crying out to the bride, "The Bridegroom is on his way."

> [7] Then all those virgins arose and trimmed their lamps.
>
> [8] And the foolish said unto the wise, 'Give us of your oil; for our lamps are gone out.'
>
> —Matthew 25:7-8

This tells you how exceptionally foolish the virgins were. The Groom Jesus is on His way, I cannot give you my oil, the Holy Spirit that lives in me, but I can tell you how to have Him live in you. Repent of your sins and receive Jesus as Lord and Savior and Holy Spirit is yours. "Mama may have, and Papa may have but God bless the child that's got his own," like the Billie Holliday song said.

Jesus is on His way back; we do not know the hour or the day. It has been over two thousand years, and the way scholars look at creation it was six days and the Father rested on the seventh day. Each day (6 days) is a thousand years (6,000 years) and Christ's millennial or 1,000-year reign is the seventh day (7,000 years total). Of course, as I mentioned before, the calendars are all wrong. The closest calendar to being correct is the Hebrew calendar and at the time of this writing it is 5,781. Only the Father knows exactly when Jesus is coming back, but time is short. 6,000 years minus 5,781 years equals 219 years remaining. What if there is less time remaining? As I said before, the calendars are all wrong. Be alert, watch and pray (1 Peter 4:7).

> But the wise answered, saying, 'Not so; lest there be not enough for us and you: but go

> ye rather to them that sell, and buy for your-
> selves.'
>
> —Matthew 25:9

The wise will not be manipulated by the world, the foolish, unsaved world which does not know God. No, go buy
for yourselves.

> And while they went to buy, the bridegroom
> came; and they that were ready went in with
> him to the marriage: and the door was shut.
>
> —Matthew 25:10 (KJV)

The door to the ark in Noah's day was shut. No one else
could board. The door to being raptured will be shut and
people will be left behind. The door to the Temple, at the
very end of the Great Tribulation, in the presence of the
Father will be shut until the seventh angel distributes the
seventh vial of the wrath of God. Do not wait until the door
is shut. Accept Jesus as Lord and Savior. He is the gift from
the Father so that the whole world would be saved. Not a
few, all the world. Receive the gift today.

> Afterward came also the other virgins, saying,
> Lord, Lord, open to us.
>
> —Matthew 25:11

The door to Noah's ark was shut. People were asking
Noah to open it. Noah did not shut it and Noah could not

open it. There will come a time when it is too late to be saved from the wrath of God. His wrath is not designed to be for people. The world was given Jesus so everyone could be saved, that they should not perish. You see the scripture does not say would not perish. You must believe in and receive the gift Jesus, accept Him as Lord and Savior and turn from sin and the Kingdom of Darkness.

> But he answered and said, Verily I say unto you, I know you not (KJV).
>
> —Matthew 25:12 (KJV)

Those people that have not persevered in the faith and are not called "overcomers" by God, will not be welcomed into heaven. How will God know?

> [20] Wherefore by their fruits ye shall know them.
>
> [21] Not everyone that saith unto me, Lord, Lord, shall enter into the kingdom of heaven; but he that doeth the will of my Father which is in heaven.
>
> [22] Many will say to me in that day, Lord, Lord, have we not prophesied in thy name? and in thy name have cast out devils? and in thy name done many wonderful works?
>
> [23] And then will I profess unto them, I never knew you: depart from me, ye that work iniquity.
>
> —Matthew 7:20-23 (KJV)

That will be an incredibly sad day. It reminds me of the movie "Left Behind" where a pastor was left behind. The senior pastor was gone. He was ranting and raving and mad at God because his wife was gone, and his children were gone. He remembered and was reminding God of all he as pastor of the church did, but he was still left behind.

> Watch therefore, for ye know neither the day nor the hour wherein the Son of man cometh.
>
> —Matthew 25:13 (KJV)

You must be ready. Watch and pray because you do not know the day. The Day of the Lord is a separate day from the catching away of the saints or the "Rapture." It is the day when Jesus returns to the earth to do battle with His enemies.

Ω

The Day of the Lord

The Old Testament prophets spoke of the day of the Lord. This is not going to be a happy day. When Jesus came the first time everyone was happy. The wise men were coming. The angels were singing, and the shepherds were excited to see the baby Jesus, Emmanuel, God with us. On the Day of the Lord, Jesus is coming back to take care of business.

> Shall not the day of the LORD be darkness,
> and not light? even very dark, and no bright-
> ness in it?
>
> —Amos 5:20 (KJV)

This is going to be a day like no other and the Lord gets revenge on His enemies and the enemies of God. Remember Eve's deception and Adam's fall. All the attacks on the Prophets, Priests and Kings of God down through history. Remember, Jesus an innocent man, beaten with a cat of nine tails, chunks of flesh coming out with each blow. Jesus was crucified, died, and was buried. He went to hell, defeated the devil, and took the keys to hell, death and the grave, and the Kingdom of Darkness no longer has the power over followers of Jesus. It is time now to collect all God's elect which includes the Old Testament saints. The real enemies of God, the antichrist, false prophet, and Satan himself, along with their followers, are the Lord's focus on the day of the Lord.

> For this is the day of the Lord GOD of hosts,
> a day of vengeance, that he may avenge him
> of his adversaries: and the sword shall de-
> vour, and it shall be satiate and made drunk
> with their blood: for the Lord GOD of hosts
> hath a sacrifice in the north country by the
> river Euphrates.
>
> —Jeremiah 46:10 (KJV)

This "sacrifice in the north country by the river Euphrates" is not your normal sacrifice. We will see it later. First, let us look at the Olivet Discourse, Matthew chapter 24, where Jesus explains the end of days to His disciples.

> And except those days should be shortened, there should no flesh be saved: but for the elect's sake those days shall be shortened.
>
> —Matthew 24:22 (KJV)

Matthew 24:22, says that no human or flesh would be saved unless the days were shortened at the end of the Great Tribulation. He then goes on to say that the days will be shortened for the "elect's sake." Who is the elect? This is the end of the Great Tribulation. The church is in heaven preparing herself for the Marriage Supper of the Lamb. The church is Jesus's elect in the New Testament, and they are gone. The Jewish remnant is God's elect in the Old Testament and God does not forget his promises to Abraham. The elect in Matthew 24:22 are the Jewish elect. So, let us look at the five things that happen on the way to the end of human government and the Millennial reign of Christ.

Armageddon – The End
Five Things That Happen on the Way to the End

FIRST: JESUS COMES TO FIGHT THE BATTLE ALONE

> Who is this who comes from Edom, with dyed garments from Bozrah *(in Edom)*, this that is glorious in his apparel, travelling in the greatness of His strength? *(Traveling triumphantly)* "I *(the Lord)* that speak in righteousness *(or proclaiming vindication)*, mighty to save."
>
> —Isaiah 63:1

Jesus is coming to free the Jewish elect from the Mountains. They have been there for 42 months or for the last 3 ½ years of 7 years, during the Great Tribulation.

> ² Wherefore art thou red in thine apparel, and thy garments like him that treadeth in the wine fat *(winepress)*?
>
> ³ I have trodden the winepress alone; and of the people there was none with me: *(Jesus goes alone to free the Jewish elect; the armies of heaven are not with him. His garments are red from blood while fighting in the battle of Armageddon.)* For I will tread them in mine anger and trample them in my fury; and their blood shall be

> sprinkled upon my garments, and I will stain all my raiment.
>
> ⁴ For the day of vengeance is in mine heart,
> And the year of my redeemed has come.
> —Isaiah 63:2-4 (KJV)

Remember, when Jesus died on the cross for our sins, He paid the price for our betrothal and our redemption. Also, remember that Holy Spirit was the down payment, the earnest paid and what sealed us until the day of redemption. Now is the day of redemption.

> And grieve not the holy Spirit of God, whereby ye are sealed unto the day of redemption.
> —Ephesians 4:30 (KJV)

For those who are born again, Jesus is our kinsman-redeemer. Boaz (a type of Jesus) in the book of Ruth, was Ruth's kinsmen-redeemer. He married Ruth and preserved the name of her father-in-law Elimelech. Jesus has purchased us with His Blood and keeps us and our names from perishing by writing us in the Lamb's Book of life. Boaz redeemed, or purchased, the family land sold by Naomi, Ruth's mother-in-law and restored it to Elimelech's line as an inheritance. The believers in Jesus have been redeemed into His eternal inheritance of "all things" including in the New Heaven and New Earth as sons and daughters of God.

> He that overcometh shall inherit all things;
> and I will be his God, and he shall be my son.
> —Revelation 21:7 (KJV)

Isaiah 63:1, explains that Jesus has come to Bozrah, in Edom, which is in Jordan today in the mountains of Petra. The question comes up, "Why does Jordan get spared from the attacks of the antichrist? Because of Psalm 108:9:

> Moab is my washpot; over Edom will I cast
> out my shoe; over Philistia will I triumph.
> —Psalms 108:9 (KJV)

Because Moab and Edom belong to God, no one will touch them.

In the first year of the tribulation, there is a seven-year peace treaty made. The two witnesses are sent by God and are there to make sure the Temple is rebuilt. At the end of the first 3 ½ years the witnesses are killed and resurrected by God. The peace treaty is broken; the antichrist called the abomination of desolation, goes into the newly reconstructed temple, and declares that he is god.

> [14] But when ye shall see the abomination of desolation, spoken of by Daniel the prophet, standing where it ought not, (let him that readeth understand,) then let them that be in Judaea flee to the mountains:

> ¹⁵ And let him that is on the housetop not go down into the house, neither enter therein, to take anything out of his house:
>
> ¹⁶ And let him that is in the field not turn back again for to take up his garment.
>
> —Mark 13:14-16 (KJV)

The Jewish elect are instructed, to flee to the mountains. They have gone to Petra in Jordan. If you Google it, you will remember it from one of the Indiana Jones movies. It is beautiful. They will hide out there until Jesus returns to get them at the end of the Great Tribulation.

> And I saw heaven opened, and behold a white horse; and he that sat upon him was called Faithful and True, and in righteousness he doth judge and make war.
>
> —Revelation 19:11

THE SECOND COMING OF JESUS CHRIST, THE DAY OF THE LORD

> His eyes were as a flame of fire, and on his head were many crowns; and he had a name written, that no man knew, but he himself.
>
> —Revelation 19:12

So, Jesus returns for the Day of the Lord to fight in the battle of Armageddon alone and frees the Jewish elect.

> Then shall the LORD go forth, and fight
> against those nations, as when he fought in
> the day of battle.
>
> —Zechariah 14:3 (KJV)

The Battle of Armageddon is Gruesome. All the people, merchants, and people from the seas that were now like clotted blood, have gathered with the antichrist in anger about the destruction of Babylon and everything else. They watch as it will be destroyed in one hour. Now they are ready to fight God himself to seek revenge. The antichrist, through many what the Bible calls "lying" wonders, which where empowered by Satan himself, have deceived them into believing that they will win this fight.

THE SACRIFICE OF THE GREAT GOD

This sacrifice refers to the Battle of Armageddon. You do not want any part of this sacrifice; you do not want to be in the opposition against God.

> And out of His mouth goeth a sharp sword,
> that with it He should smite the nations: and
> He shall rule them with a rod of iron: and He
> treadeth the winepress of the fierceness and
> wrath of Almighty God.
>
> —Revelation 19:15

Those gathered are evil. Revelation 19:15 should let everyone know that believes the love of God will prevent Him from destroying His enemies, realize they are wrong. God also hates sin and punishes the wicked. When it says, "He shall rule them with a rod of iron:" that means He will destroy them with the "wrath of Almighty God".

> [16] And he hath on his vesture and on his thigh a name written, KING OF KINGS, AND LORD OF LORDS.
> [17] And I saw an angel standing in the sun; and he cried with a loud voice, saying to all the fowls that fly in the midst of heaven, Come and gather yourselves together unto the supper of the great God;
> *This is the sacrifice.*
> [18] That ye may eat the flesh of kings, and the flesh of captains, and the flesh of mighty men, and the flesh of horses, and of them that sit on them, and the flesh of all men, both free and bond, both small and great.
> —Revelation 19:16-18

Nothing will save the wicked. Their money will not save them. Their status in life will not save them.

> [19] And I saw the beast *(the antichrist)*, and the kings of the earth, and their armies, gathered together to make war against him that sat on the horse, and against his army.
> [20] And the beast was taken, and with him the false prophet that wrought miracles be-

> fore him, with which he deceived them that
> had received the mark of the beast *(Satan),*
> and them that worshipped his image. These
> both were cast alive into a lake of fire burning
> with brimstone.
>
> —Revelation 19:19-20

The antichrist and the false prophet were immediately cast into the lake of fire where Satan was not. Satan is first cast into the bottomless pit as we will see later.

It is this scripture that should remind everyone to look at both sides of every issue so that you will not be among the deceived. Trust in the Lord. Lean not to your own understanding. In all your ways acknowledge God and He will direct you into the God path. Otherwise, you could be deceived by what you hear or see. You must go by what God says. Ask for wisdom and direction. Seek God and you will find Him. Knock and God's door will be opened. (Luke 11:9) The Truth is found in the Word. The written Word of God is the Bible. As you read the Bible the Bible will read you, determine your needs and God will speak to you. (Hebrews 4:12)

> And the remnant *(of the wicked)* were slain
> with the sword of him that sat upon the horse,
> which sword proceeded out of his mouth:
> and all the fowls were filled with their flesh.
>
> —Revelation 19:21 (KJV)

SECOND: JESUS GOES BACK TO HEAVEN TO GET THE ARMIES OF HEAVEN

First, was Jesus coming to earth to fight the battle alone. Second, Jesus goes back to heaven to get the armies of heaven and comes down on a white horse.

> And He was clothed with a vesture dipped in blood: and His name is called The Word of God.
>
> —Revelation 19:13 (KJV)

Jesus is His earthly name. The Word is His eternal Name.

> [1] In the beginning was the Word, and the Word was with God, and the Word was God.
> [2] The same was in the beginning with God.
> [3] All things were made by him; and without him was not anything made that was made.
> [4] In him was life; and the life was the light of men.
> [5] And the light shineth in darkness; and the darkness comprehended it not *(or received it not).*
>
> —John 1:1-5 (KJV)

His clothes appeared dipped in blood because He had been fighting in the battle of Armageddon (Revelation 19:13).

Jesus is on a white horse and all the armies are on white horses as they come to earth.

> And the armies which were in heaven followed Him upon white horses, clothed in fine linen, white and clean.
> —Revelation 19:14 (KJV)

There are four groups that make up the armies of heaven. First is the Bride of Christ, the church. Second is all the believers saved in the tribulation called the Tribulation Saints. Third is all the godly Old Testament saints resurrected to everlasting life at the end of the Tribulation found in Daniel 12:1-2. The fourth group is the holy angels with the Son of man, Jesus, when He comes into His glory found in Matthew 25:31. Note that the white horses are not regular white horses found on earth they are from heaven. (MacArthur 2007)

THIRD: JESUS AND THE ARMIES OF HEAVEN GO TO THE MOUNT OF OLIVES

Jesus returns from heaven with the armies of heaven and arrive at the Mount of Olives.

> And his feet shall stand in that day upon the mount of Olives, which is before Jerusalem

> on the east, and the mount of Olives shall cleave in the midst thereof toward the east and toward the west, and there shall be a very great valley; and half of the mountain shall remove toward the north, and half of it toward the south.
>
> —Zechariah 14:4 (KJV)

When Jesus's feet touch down onto the Mount of Olives the mountain splits. Half the water under the temple mount flows into the Mediterranean and the other half flows into the Dead Sea and it is given life. The house described below is the Temple Mount.

> Afterward he brought me again unto the door of the house; and, behold, waters issued out from under the threshold of the house eastward: for the forefront of the house stood toward the east, and the waters came down from under from the right side of the house, at the south side of the altar
>
> —Ezekiel 47:1 (KJV)

> 8 Then said He unto me, 'These waters issue out toward the east country, and go down into the desert, and go into the sea: which being brought forth into the sea, the waters shall be healed.

⁹ And it shall come to pass, that everything that liveth, which moveth, whithersoever the rivers *(two)* shall come, shall live: and there shall be a very great multitude of fish, because these waters shall come thither: for they shall be healed; and everything shall live whither the river cometh.

¹⁰ And it shall come to pass, that the fishers shall stand upon it from Engedi even unto Eneglaim; they shall be a place to spread forth nets; their fish shall be according to their kinds, as the fish of the great sea, exceeding many'.

—Ezekiel 47:8-10 (KJV)

And by the river upon the bank thereof, on this side and on that side, shall grow all trees for meat, whose leaf shall not fade, neither shall the fruit thereof be consumed: it shall bring forth new fruit according to his months, because their waters they issued out of the sanctuary: and the fruit thereof shall be for meat, and the leaf thereof for medicine.

—Ezekiel 47:12 (KJV)

Everything the rivers touch that flow from the Mount of Olives after it splits shall live and provide for life and healing during the Millennial reign of Jesus.

FOURTH: EVERY KNEE SHALL BOW
AND EVERY TONGUE SHALL CONFESS

Before Satan is put in the bottomless pit. He bows his knee and confesses that Jesus is Lord.

---

[21] Tell ye, and bring them near; yea, let them take counsel together: who hath declared this from ancient time? Who hath told it from that time? Have not I the LORD? And there is no God else beside me; a just God and a Savior; there is none beside me.

[22] Look unto me, and be ye saved, all the ends of the earth: for I am God, and there is none else.

[23] I have sworn by myself, the word is gone out of my mouth in righteousness, and shall not return, That unto me every knee shall bow, every tongue shall swear.

—Isaiah 45:21-23 (KJV)

---

[8] And being found in fashion as a man, he humbled himself, and became obedient unto death, even the death of the cross.

[9] Wherefore God also hath highly exalted him, and given him a name which is above every name:

[10] That at the name of Jesus every knee should bow, of things in heaven, and things in earth, and things under the earth. *(That in-*

> *cludes everything and everyone in heaven, earth, and hell.)*
>
> [11] And that every tongue should confess that Jesus Christ is Lord, to the glory of God the Father.
>
> —Philippians 2:8-11 (KJV)

The final judgement for the wicked is yet to take place. The people with their names written in the Lambs book of life have already been judged at this point and they know their rewards.

FIFTH: SATAN IS BOUND FOR 1,000 YEARS

> [1] And I saw an angel come down from heaven, having the key of the bottomless pit and a great chain in his hand.
>
> [2] And he laid hold on the dragon, that old serpent, which is the Devil, and Satan, and bound him a thousand years,
>
> [3] And cast him into the bottomless pit, and shut him up, and set a seal upon him, that he should deceive the nations no more, till the thousand years should be fulfilled: and after that he must be loosed a little season.
>
> —Revelation 20:1-3 (KJV)

The devil was shut up physically but also his mouth was shut up. Everything he says is a lie. He is the father of lies. Can you imagine falling and falling and falling for a thousand years. There is no bottom to the bottomless pit. It is interesting that he will be released after a thousand years. After the 1,000 year, or Millennial reign, of Jesus. That is the little season. There will be people that come out of the Tribulation alive that do not fight against Jesus in the Battle of Armageddon. They and their children must accept Jesus as Lord during this "little season."

THE LAST DAY OF THE TRIBULATION/ THE FIRST DAY OF THE MILLENNIAL REIGN OF JESUS

On the last day of the Tribulation, (which is the first day of the Millennial Reign of Jesus) there will be a great upheaval of nature. The earth shall move out of her place due to the violent earthquakes. Scholars believe that maybe it is a move back to where it was prior to sin coming on the earth during Adam's time.

> Therefore I will shake the heavens, and the earth shall remove out of her place, in the wrath of the LORD of hosts, and in the day of his fierce anger.
> —Isaiah 13:13 (KJV)

It will be neither day nor night, but at evening it will be light.

> [6] And it shall come to pass in that day, that the light shall not be clear, nor dark:

> ⁷ But it shall be one day which shall be known to the LORD, not day, nor night: but it shall come to pass, that at evening time it shall be light.
>
> —Zechariah 14:6-7

Jesus is the Light. The believers are the saints in the Light.

> ¹² Giving thanks unto the Father, which hath made us meet to be partakers of the inheritance of the saints in light:
>
> ¹³ Who hath delivered us from the power of darkness, and hath translated us into the kingdom of his dear Son.
>
> —Colossians 1:12-13 (KJV)

Believers have been delivered from the dominion of Satan and are now in the Kingdom of God through our relationship with Jesus Christ.

In that day, the last day of the Great Tribulation, the last day of the world system of government, on the Day of the Lord, Jesus will be King and Lord over all the earth.

> ⁸ And it shall be in that day, that living waters shall go out from Jerusalem; half of them toward the former *(or Eastern)* sea, and half of them toward the hinder sea: in summer and in winter shall it be.

> [9] And the LORD shall be king over all the earth: in that day shall there be one LORD, and his name one.
>
> —Zechariah 14:8-9 (KJV)

In that day, we shall be "one" for real, in the Name of Jesus. Amen.

CHAPTER 12

The Beginning: and the Government Shall Be Upon His Shoulder; the 1,000 Year Reign & the New Heaven and Earth

> For unto us a child is born, unto us a son is given: and the government shall be upon his shoulder: and his name shall be called Wonderful, Counsellor, The mighty God, The everlasting Father, The Prince of Peace.
> —Isaiah 9:6 (KJV)

The first half of that prophecy in Isaiah 9:6 was fulfilled over two thousand years ago with the birth of Jesus. Now it is time for Jesus to take His rightful place as King and Lord of all. John tells us about it in Revelation 20:4.

> And I saw thrones, and they sat upon them, and judgment was given unto them: and I saw the souls of them that were beheaded for the witness of Jesus, and for the word of God,

> and which had not worshipped the beast, nei-
> ther his image, neither had received his mark
> upon their foreheads, or in their hands; and
> they lived and reigned with Christ a thousand
> years.
>
> —Revelation 20:4 (KJV)

Ω

The Millennial Reign of Jesus Christ

This time is being looked for, waited for, and sought after by the people of God for almost six thousand years now. No more wars or rumors of wars. Peace beyond all understanding.

Ω

Jesus Has Everlasting Dominion

Jesus finally has begun to walk in the dominion given to Adam and turned over to Satan.

> I saw in the night visions, and, behold, one
> like the Son of man came with the clouds of
> heaven, and came to the Ancient of days, and
> they brought Him near before Him.
>
> —Daniel 7:13 (KJV)

Daniel saw it as a vision, an open vision where Daniel experienced being there. He saw Jesus as described in Daniel 7:14.

> And there was given Him dominion, and glory, and a kingdom, that all people, nations, and languages, should serve Him: His dominion is an everlasting dominion, which shall not pass away, and His kingdom that which shall not be destroyed.
>
> —Daniel 7:14 (KJV)

A place where all people, from every nation, creed, and color serves Jesus. The Jesus that loves us this we know, for the Bible tells us so. And for the people who do not understand what the Bible really is, let us look at the acronym B.I.B.L.E. which is Basic Instructions Before Leaving Earth. It is a book of truth that if read day and night and night and day, will renew your mind to understand the truth contained within.

War No More Or Fear

In the present we live with a constant pressure of possible war. Somewhere in the world there is war, even now. In the Kingdom of God, where Jesus is King of the Kingdom, we are citizens now with the "new birth" or being born again into the family of God. Our names are written into the Lambs Book of Life. We are on earth doing what our Father has planned for us until we have finished our course and our race is done. Good and faithful servants to the end.

> [3] And he shall judge among many people, and rebuke strong nations afar off; and they shall beat their swords into plowshares, and their spears into pruninghooks: nation shall not lift up a sword against nation, neither shall they learn war anymore.
>
> [4] But they shall sit every man under his vine and under his fig tree; and none shall make them afraid: for the mouth of the LORD of hosts hath spoken it.
>
> —Micah 4:3-4 (KJV)

Ω

Jesus Will Share His Reign

> And he that overcometh, and keepeth my works unto the end, to him will I give power over the nations:
>
> —Revelation 2:26

During this 1,000-year reign we will be on earth, not in heaven. In our glorified bodies we will serve Jesus in whatever capacity He asks us. Others which are saved out of the Great Tribulation will be those who repopulate the earth.

> And he shall rule them with a rod of iron; as the vessels of a potter shall they be broken to shivers: even as I received of my Father.
> —Revelation 2:27 (KJV)

WITH HIS BRIDE

> [9] And they sung a new song, saying, 'Thou art worthy *(speaking of Jesus)* to take the book, and to open the seals thereof: for thou wast slain, and hast redeemed us to God by thy blood out of every kindred, and tongue, and people, and nation;
> [10] And hast made us unto our God kings and priests: and we shall reign on the earth.
> —Revelation 5:9-10 (KJV)

We are the chosen people, the royal priesthood that will reign on earth with Jesus (1 Peter 2:9).

WITH THE OLD TESTAMENT SAINTS

These Old Testament saints paved the way for the birth of Jesus to a people, the Children of Israel, and others who are found in Hebrews chapter 11, the Hall of Faith.

> [37] They were stoned, they were sawn asunder, were tempted, were slain with the sword: they

wandered about in sheepskins and goatskins; being destitute, afflicted, tormented;

38 *(Of whom the world was not worthy:)* they wandered in deserts, and in mountains, and in dens and caves of the earth.

39 And these all, having obtained a good report through faith, received not the promise:

40 God having provided some better thing for us, that they without us should not be made perfect.

—Hebrews 11:37-40 (KJV)

The Old Testament saints obtained a good report of faith but never received the promise. But they paved the way for those who came afterwards, chosen by God to finish their work.

WITH THOSE WITNESSES
AND THOSE MARTYRED IN THE TRIBULATION

13 And one of the elders answered, saying unto me, 'What are these which are arrayed in white robes? and whence came they?'

14 And I said unto him,' Sir, thou knowest.' And he said to me, 'These are they which came out of great tribulation, and have washed their robes, and made them white in the blood of the Lamb.

—Revelation 7:13-14 (KJV)

There Will Be Joy and No Crying

And I will rejoice in Jerusalem, and joy in my people: and the voice of weeping shall be no more heard in her, nor the voice of crying

—Isaiah 65:19 (KJV)

The People on Earth That Are Ruled

THOSE WHO SURVIVED THE GREAT TRIBULATION AND WERE FAITHFUL TO JESUS CHRIST

And I heard another voice from heaven, saying, 'Come out of her *(Babylon)*, my people, that ye be not partakers of her sins, and that ye receive not of her plagues'.

—Revelation 18:4 (KJV)

THOSE BORN DURING THE MILLENNIAL REIGN OF CHRIST FROM THOSE WHO SURVIVED THE GREAT TRIBULATION

There shall be no more thence an infant of days, nor an old man that hath not filled his days: for the child shall die an hundred years old; but the sinner being an hundred years old shall be accursed

—Isaiah 65:20 (KJV)

Ω

Animals and Nature are Restored to God's Original Design (Except for the Serpent)

The wolf and the lamb shall feed together, and the lion shall eat straw like the bullock: and dust shall be the serpent's meat. They shall not hurt nor destroy in all my holy mountain, saith the LORD.

—Isaiah 65:25 (KJV)

And the LORD God said unto the serpent, 'Because thou hast done this, thou art cursed above all cattle, and above every beast of the field; upon thy belly shalt thou go, and dust shalt thou eat all the days of thy life:

—Genesis 3:14 (KJV)

[8] But ye, O mountains of Israel, ye shall shoot forth your branches, and yield your fruit to my people of Israel; for they are at hand to come.

⁹ For, behold, I am for you, and I will turn unto you, and ye shall be tilled and sown:

¹⁰ And I will multiply men upon you, all the house of Israel, even all of it: and the cities shall be inhabited, and the wastes shall be builded:

¹¹ And I will multiply upon you man and beast; and they shall increase and bring fruit: and I will settle you after your old estates and will do better unto you than at your beginnings: and ye shall know that I am the LORD.

—Ezekiel 36:8-11 (KJV)

Ω

End of the 1,000 Year Millennial Reign

BLESSED ARE THOSE THAT HAVE PART IN THE 1ST RESURRECTION

Those that are born again into the family of God are saved from the second death.

⁵ But the rest of the dead lived not again until the thousand years were finished. This is the first resurrection.

⁶ Blessed and holy is he that hath part in the first resurrection: on such the second death hath no power, but they shall be priests

of God and of Christ, and shall reign with
him a thousand years.

—Revelation 20:5-6 (KJV)

SATAN IS RELEASED FROM THE BOTTOMLESS PIT WHEN THE 1,000 YEARS HAVE ENDED

It is amazing that people who have experienced the 1,000-year reign of Christ will choose to abandon the faith and gather to battle against Jesus.

7 And when the thousand years are expired, Satan shall be loosed out of his prison,

8 And shall go out to deceive the nations which are in the four quarters of the earth, Gog and Magog, to gather them together to battle: the number of whom is as the sand of the sea.

—Revelation 20:7-8 (KJV)

Ω

This Is the Last Rebellion: Revelation 20:8-9

And they went up on the breadth of the earth, and compassed the camp of the saints about,

> and the beloved city: and fire came down
> from God out of heaven and devoured them
> —Revelation 20:9 (KJV)

There is no fighting, just fire from heaven to destroy them.

SATAN IS PUNISHED ETERNALLY

Finally, Satan is cast into the Lake of Fire where the anti-christ and false prophet is. Satan is there to be tormented, burning alive in the fire forever.

> And the devil that deceived them was cast
> into the lake of fire and brimstone, where the
> beast and the false prophet are, and shall be
> tormented day and night for ever and ever.
> —Revelation 20:10 (KJV)

The Great White Throne Judgement

This is the time of the final judgement of the unsaved that have ever lived on earth.

> And I saw a great white throne, and him that
> sat on it, from whose face the earth and the
> heaven fled away; and there was found no
> place for them.
> —Revelation 20:11 (KJV)

THE BOOKS ARE OPENED

There are two types of books. God's books have every person that has ever lived on earth in it. The second type of book is The Lamb's Book of Life with the names of those people that are born again into the family of God. Those that have accepted Jesus as their personal Lord and Savior.

THE DEAD ARE JUDGED

[12] And I saw the dead, small and great, stand before God; and the books were opened: and another book was opened, which is the book of life: and the dead were judged out of those things which were written in the books, according to their works.

[13] And the sea gave up the dead which were in it; and death and hell delivered up the dead which were in them: and they were judged every man according to their works.

—Revelation 20:12-13 (KJV)

DEATH AND HELL ARE CAST INTO THE LAKE OF FIRE ALONG WITH EVERYONE NOT FOUND IN THE LAMB'S BOOK OF LIFE

[14] And death and hell were cast into the lake of fire. This is the second death.

Monoseta Burwell

> ¹⁵ And whosoever was not found written in the book of life was cast into the lake of fire.
>
> —Revelation 20:14-15 (KJV)

THE SECOND DEATH

The people who are born again die once but live twice. Those that are not born again live once and die twice. They experience the second death.

Ω

Anyone Not Found in the Lamb's Book of Life Is Cast into the Lake of Fire

THOSE WHO HAVE REJECTED JESUS CHRIST AND HAVE CHOSEN TO PERISH

> For God so loved the world, that he gave his only begotten Son, that whosoever believeth in him should not perish, but have everlasting life.
>
> —John 3:16 (KJV)

The Father gave His only Son as a gift, a sacrifice so that we should not perish. But we must receive or accept this gift.

> And he that sat upon the throne said, Behold, I make all things new. And he said unto me, 'Write: for these words are true and faithful.'
>
> —Revelation 21:5 (KJV)

THIS IS JESUS ON THE THRONE OF GOD HIS FATHER SPEAKING.

> [6] And He said unto me, 'It is done. I am Alpha and Omega, the beginning and the end. I will give unto him that is athirst of the fountain of the water of life freely.
>
> [7] He that overcometh shall inherit all things; and I will be his God, and he shall be my son.
>
> [8] But the fearful, and unbelieving, and the abominable, and murderers, and whoremongers, and sorcerers, and idolaters, and all liars, shall have their part in the lake which burneth with fire and brimstone: which is the second death'
>
> —Revelation 21:6-8 (KJV)

JESUS DELIVERS THE KINGDOM TO THE FATHER

---

24 Then cometh the end, when He shall have delivered up the kingdom to God, even the Father; when He shall have put down all rule and all authority and power.

25 For He must reign, till He hath put all enemies under His feet.

26 The last enemy that shall be destroyed is death.

27 For He hath put all things under His feet. But when He saith all things are put under Him, it is manifest that He is excepted, which did put all things under Him.

28 And when all things shall be subdued unto Him, then shall the Son also Himself be subject unto Him that put all things under Him, that God may be all in all.

—I Corinthians 15:24-28 (KJV)

When everything is totally under the control of the Son, the Lamb of God, Jesus then takes it all, including Himself and puts it under the authority of the Father God.

THEN BEGINS THE EVERLASTING KINGDOM OF GOD AND THE LAMB.
THE OLD PASSES AWAY AND GOD CREATES A NEW HEAVEN AND A NEW EARTH

> [1] And I saw a new heaven and a new earth: for the first heaven and the first earth were passed away; and there was no more sea.
>
> [2] And I John saw the holy city, new Jerusalem, coming down from God out of heaven, prepared as a bride adorned for her husband.
>
> [3] And I heard a great voice out of heaven saying, Behold, the tabernacle of God is with men, and he will dwell with them, and they shall be his people, and God himself shall be with them, and be their God
>
> —Revelation 21:1-3 (KJV)

And we shall dwell in the House of the Lord forever and ever.

> [22] And I saw no temple therein: for the Lord God Almighty and the Lamb are the temple of it.
>
> [23] And the city had no need of the sun, neither of the moon, to shine in it: for the glory of God did lighten it, and the Lamb is the light thereof.

Monoseta Burwell

> ²⁴ And the nations of them which are saved shall walk in the light of it: and the kings of the earth do bring their glory and honour into it.
>
> —Revelation 21:22-24 (KJV)

All those born again into the family of God are the royal priesthood, the kings of the earth.

> ²⁵ And the gates of it shall not be shut at all by day: for there shall be no night there.
>
> ²⁶ And they shall bring the glory and honour of the nations into it.
>
> —Revelation 21:25-26 (KJV)

Only the born again shall enter the New Heaven and the New Earth.

> And there shall in no wise enter into it anything that defileth, neither whatsoever worketh abomination, or maketh a lie: but they which are written in the Lamb's book of life.
>
> —Revelation 21:27 (KJV)

¹ And He shewed me a pure river of water of life, clear as crystal, proceeding out of the throne of God and of the Lamb.

² In the midst of the street of it, and on either side of the river, was there the tree of life, which bare twelve manner of fruits, and yielded her fruit every month: and the leaves of the tree were for the healing of the nations.

³ And there shall be no more curse: but the throne of God and of the Lamb shall be in it; and His servants shall serve Him:

⁴ And they shall see His face; and His name shall be in their foreheads.

⁵ And there shall be no night there; and they need no candle, neither light of the sun; for the Lord God giveth them light: and they shall reign for ever and ever.

—Revelation 22:1-5 (KJV)

Ω

Praise the Lord! A Word from Jesus

¹² And, behold, I come quickly; and my reward is with me, to give every man according as his work shall be.

¹³ I am Alpha and Omega, the beginning and the end, the first and the last.

¹⁴ Blessed are they that do His commandments, that they may have right to the tree of life and may enter in through the gates into the city.

¹⁵ For without are dogs, and sorcerers, and whoremongers, and murderers, and idolaters, and whosoever loveth and maketh a lie.

¹⁶ I Jesus have sent mine angel to testify unto you these things in the churches. I am the root and the offspring of David, and the bright and morning star.

¹⁷ And the Spirit and the bride say, Come. And let him that heareth say, Come. And let him that is athirst come. And whosoever will, let him take the water of life freely.

—Revelation 22:12-17 (KJV)

Ω

John: "Come, Lord Jesus"

He which testifieth these things saith, Surely I come quickly. Amen. Even so, come, Lord Jesus.

—Revelation 22:20 (KJV)

So, tonight, pick up your Bible and turn to the book of Revelation and start reading it from the beginning. It is the Revelation of our Lord and Savior Jesus Christ. You will be blessed. This book cannot replace Revelation. This book will help you to place the End-Times in an order that may be more understandable in this present time.

> He which testifieth these things saith, Surely, I come quickly. Amen. Even so, come, Lord Jesus.
>
> —Revelation 22:20 (KJV)

Ω

What Should We Do While We Wait?

What should we be doing while we wait for the beginning of the end? That question brings us back to today.

What Should We Do While We Wait?

Step Out in Faith and Live the Life God Designed!

> The steps of a good man are ordered by the LORD: and he delighteth in His way.
>
> —Psalms 37:23 (KJV)

> [13] For thou hast possessed my reins *(my inward thoughts and desires)*: thou hast covered me in my mother's womb *(from the moment of conception)*.
>
> [14] I will praise thee; for I am fearfully and wonderfully made: marvellous are thy works; and that my soul knoweth right well.
>
> —Psalms 139:13-14 (KJV)

This book is about the end-times, but our Father in heaven wants you not to focus so much on the end of life as we know it, but to focus on preparing for the beginning of life lived in the presence of God in His Kingdom. This begins with being born again into God's family as a son or daughter of His. A good man in Psalms 37:23 is a man that is a son or daughter of God.

Ω

God Designed Us for This Life

Stepping out in faith while we wait on the future God designed for us is not easy. We live in a world filled with chaos. Just turn on the news at any moment and you will see this chaos in living color. It does not matter what political party you belong to. After the election you have half the country against just about everything you believe in. More and more today unlike in the past, after the election the country remains divided. A house divided cannot stand. The church, the body of Christ, should not be divided. We should walk in unity with God as the head of the church.

> And if a house be divided against itself, that house cannot stand.
> —Mark 3:25 (KJV)

We have been warned in the prophesy from Jesus in Matthew 24 that things will get worse and worse including moral decay and spiritual decay, enhanced by the deception of false prophets. Our job will be to endure until the end and when we have done all just stand on the Word of God, our only offensive weapon, fully clothed in the armor of God our only protection.

> But let us, who are of the day, be sober, putting on the breastplate of faith and love; and for an helmet, the hope of salvation.
>
> —1 Thessalonians 5:8 (KJV)

We sons and daughters of God are "of the day" which precedes the night of the wrath of God to come on the Day of the Lord. We are to be sober which has more than one meaning. Avoiding mind altering substances that could prevent your mind from being alert to what is going on is one meaning and being alert spiritually remaining prayerful, diligently seeking, and abiding in God daily for instruction and guidance is the other meaning.

The breastplate of faith is a shield to guard our heart to remain steadfast in whom we trust, and in whose Word we trust, remembering our Father who is love and who loves us. This will keep us focused to repel the fiery darts of the enemy which will come to deceive us, take our focus off God, to set us up to steal the Word of God, kill God's plans for our destiny, and ultimately destroy us.

> [9] For God hath not appointed us to wrath, but to obtain salvation by our Lord Jesus Christ,
>
> [10] Who died for us, that, whether we wake or sleep, we should live together with him.
>
> [11] Wherefore comfort yourselves together, and edify one another, even as also ye do.
>
> —1 Thessalonians 5:9-11 (KJV)

So, while we wait for Jesus to return to rule and reign triumphantly, we need to put aside all the chaos in the world. Comfort, edify, and exhort your brothers and sisters in the Lord. The world will not do this. The saints of God must do this. Look up (towards heaven,) stand up (for the things of God,) cheer up (be joyful because the joy of the Lord is our strength,) and step out in faith and live the life God designed.

At the time of writing this chapter, the whole world is in the grips of the Corona Virus, COVID-19. People are dying in biblical proportions. Many Christians vividly see Matthew 24:7 with the Corona Virus pestilence. It has taken the world by surprise. Even the treatment of it has put people at risk because there is no known cure. Every possible treatment that is tested becomes controversial and political while more and more people die. A vaccine is on the way, but some are even hesitant to even take it. Some people question the side effects of the vaccine.

We are seeing an increase in earthquakes over the world and even in rare places. Hurricane activity is greater than ever before. So much so that they have even run out of names in the alphabet. Some hurricanes have hit in new ways like two days apart with Marco and Laura, which were even considered un-survivable. When will it all end? No one knows for sure. Therefore, our focus must be placed on God for help, not man. Our source is God not the news media. We must pray and ask God for His wisdom, His understanding, His clarity. Our faith and trust should be in God not the government. Our Lord and Savior Jesus has conquered even death, so trust God and fear not.

> [6] And ye shall hear of wars and rumours of wars: see that ye be not troubled: for all these things must come to pass, but the end is not yet.
>
> [7] For nation shall rise against nation, and kingdom against kingdom: and there shall be famines, and pestilences, and earthquakes, in divers places.
>
> —Matthew 24:6-7 (KJV)

Then with the death of an African American man by the name of George Floyd, literally by the knee of a police officer, many protested but many, against the wishes of the family, rioted using Mr. Floyd's name. We saw nation rising against nation, or ethnic group against ethnic group. A new nation formed rising against the United States, called CHAZ later changing its name to CHOP right in the middle of, Seattle, Washington, a U.S. city, until it was disbanded. Grocery store shelves emptied. Amazingly, toilet paper became scarce. Food lines formed for miles in just about every state at some point or another, a sign that famine was in the land.

One thing we must remember, the Corona Virus does not possess the final crown. The person that wears the final crown has a Name above Corona or COVID-19, or any other number including 666 for that matter. He is the King of kings and the Lord of lords. His Name is Jesus. He not only owns the earth and they that dwell there in (Psalms 24:1), He is the creator of the earth and that makes Him the Lord of all lords. And now we know that Jesus reigns supreme. Chapter 1-11 has reviewed the basics of it all. When everything is said and done, God our Father, who loves us all, sent His Son to save us and the whole world. At the end of Chapter 11 you can see that Jesus will win. Because He wins, we win. Thank you, Jesus. Remember God does everything from the end to the beginning. So, we have already won.

> That which hath been is now; and that which is to be hath already been; and God requireth that which is past.
>
> —Ecclesiastes 3:15 (KJV)

Through all of what is happening on earth while we wait for Jesus, we must stay prayed up, have faith, and let our steps be ordered by the Lord, not by the chaos around us. We must believe in our covenant relationship with God through Jesus, our Lord and Savior. Jesus is the only way, the only truth, and the only life for us to pursue especially in this or any time of chaos. We must not lose our focus on God.

We must have faith in our Father that designed us and trust Him to bring His plan for our lives to pass. It will not be easy, but it will be impossible without God. We must put our hand in God's hand. Let Him lead the way, His way, "The steps of a good man are ordered by the Lord." And God delights in us following His way.

> For thou hast possessed my reins: thou hast covered me in my mother's womb.
> —Psalms 139:13 (KJV)

God formed us in our mother's womb. He formed our thoughts and desires at that time. He was actively involved in all that from the moment of conception. From the moment of conception God had a plan for our lives.

> I will praise thee; for I am fearfully and wonderfully made: marvellous are thy works; and that my soul knoweth right well.
> —Psalms 139:14 (KJV)

We are fearfully or reverently and wonderfully made. Think of that. Normally, it is God that we hold in reverence. But God feels that way about us. And we are wonderfully made. Only a loving Father would take such care and such concern. Then we, thinking of it, can be excited like David and say, "marvellous are thy works." "I am fearfully and wonderfully made."

Think of this as you reflect on just how marvelous God's works are. I mentioned this in the beginning of the book. My mind can hardly grasp this:

- Man was created so that God, as baby Jesus could be carried in and born from a human being, His mother, the Virgin Mary.
- Man was created so that God, as the Holy Spirit could reside in us, all the born-again human beings at the same time.

Amazing. Marvelous are God's works. We are truly fearfully and wonderfully made.

> My substance was not hid from thee, when I was made in secret, and curiously wrought in the lowest parts of the earth.
> —Psalms 139:15 (KJV)

"My substance," including my purpose, was curiously or skillfully and intricately "wrought" or designed in "the lowest parts of the earth" or a place of mystery.

Think of the people you know that have come into your life. Think of how you met your spouse and your close friends. Think of the design of everything that is happening in your life, all your interactions, your college friends, even the church you have joined, the ministries you serve on and the people there, your place of employment and how all of that has seemingly fallen into place. It is like a Tapestry, your life embroidered or fabricated to include you in their purpose and them in yours.

When my husband and I were Pastors a couple came to the church and were married by my husband. As they were there for a while, they wanted to find a way to serve the church. They had an idea of bringing a Leadership Training Program to the church. My husband thanked them and told them maybe later but now he needed people on Audio and Ushers. They were willing and obedient. Dr. Steven Jones, who later revealed that he was a minister, began to learn all about the Audio ministry. He and his wife Mrs. Stacey Jones both joined the Usher and Greeters Ministry. Dr. Steven Jones later became the Assistant Executive Minister and worked diligently, helping the Executive Minister, Evangelist Belinda Hildreth Thompson, who was our right hand.

About three years later, in January of 2019 when my husband and I announced that we were retiring, we had a minister's meeting immediately following the service. We asked if anyone was led to start a church. Dr. Steven Jones stated that he had been led to start a church. We told him to go talk to his wife and they pray about it. He came back after they had prayed and told us that he would like to start a church. We elevated Dr. Jones to Pastor later that month. We gave him everything including the chairs, pulpits, and audio. The week after our final service we all went to worship at their new church.

The first week the church opened they were in a hotel. The hotel audio did not work properly. Dr. Jones did not know that was going to happen, but God had prepared him in advance. He knew how to hook his audio up to replace the hotel's, so everything worked well. They had been trained for excellence and they were prepared to still have church when things went wrong.

When I took over the Women's Ministry, I had no idea how I was going to manage it by myself with my full-time dental practice and being Pastor. I asked for a volunteer to help me as Chairperson. Mrs. Stacey Jones volunteered. This was a big help for me and in case you are beginning to see God's Tapestry unfold here, it was a part of God's design. The rest of God's design was that being the Chairperson of the Women's Ministry, it allowed Stacey to have an opportunity to get to know all the women in the church. It also allowed all the women in the church to get to know her. Little did she know that she would be the First Lady of their new church. So, when they opened the church and asked people to come and join them, the women already had a relationship with her and were willing to help.

Our purpose was skillfully and intricately designed like a Tapestry. Fabricated to include the Jones family in our purpose and to include us in their purpose. All designed by God for the relationships that formed and continue to this day. Also, for the continuance of the church and the family of believers that had served together for many years.

> Thine eyes did see my substance *(my everything)* yet being unperfect *(or unformed)*; and in thy book all my members were written, which in continuance *(all my days)* were fashioned *(or designed for me)*, when as yet there was none of them *(before I was born)*.
> —Psalms 137:16 (KJV)

Before we were born, we were designed completely, in our mother's womb. We have been fearfully and wonderfully made. Designed by God Himself.

So, I have two questions for you:

- God designed your life; are you living it?
- Are you following the orders and taking the steps?

> The steps of a good man are ordered *(or ordained)* by the LORD: and he delighteth in His way.
>
> —Psalms 37:23 (KJV)

There are two ways of doing things. The way of the world or the way of God. The world system, our flesh, and the way we think if using the world system, will prevent us from following the orders, taking the steps, and living the life God designed for us. Some people are skipping steps. Even if we are saved or born again. We are supposed to be in the world (we live in it) but we are not supposed to be of, or a part of, the world system.

> For to be carnally *(flesh)* minded is death; but to be spiritually minded *(following the Word of God)* is life and peace.
>
> —Romans 8:6 (KJV)

The mind controls the body.

> [7] Because the carnal mind *(unsaved, not born again or unrenewed mind)* is enmity *(at war)*

> against God: for it is not subject to the law of God, neither indeed can be.
>
> [8] So then they that are in the flesh cannot please God.
>
> —Romans 8:7-8 (KJV)

So, what we need to know is the following:

- We are born in this world.
- We are born with a carnal mind.
- We are born with a spirit that is separated from God (a dead spirit.) That is because:
  - Adam, against God's will for him, ate the fruit of the tree of knowledge of good and evil and it produced a genetic flaw that introduced sin and death into the whole world.
  - He died spiritually from eating that fruit. All his offspring (all humans) also are born with this genetic flaw. But being born again, we are regenerated (or regened), we are new creatures in Christ. Jesus Christ has made us free from the law of sin and death.

> Wherefore, as by one man sin entered into the world, and death by sin; and so death passed upon all men, for that all have sinned.
>
> —Romans 5:12 (KJV)

Therefore if any man be in Christ, he is a new creature: old things are passed away; behold, all things are become new.

—2 Corinthians 5:17 (KJV)

[1] There is therefore now no condemnation to them which are in Christ Jesus, who walk not after the flesh, but after the Spirit.

[2] For the law of the Spirit of life in Christ Jesus hath made me free from the law of sin and death.

—Romans 8:1-2 (KJV)

- We are spirit beings, we live in a body and we possess a soul, which is our mind, will, and emotions.
- We are not human beings living a spiritual experience. We are spirit beings living a human experience.

I beseech you therefore, brethren, by the mercies of God, that ye present your bodies *(this flesh suit)* a living sacrifice *(a living offering)*, holy, *(a set aside life that is)* acceptable unto God, which is your reasonable service.

—Romans 12:1 (KJV)

Why is this our reasonable service? Because we have been bought for a price, "every kindred, tongue, people and nation," were purchased by the blood of Jesus. The whole world was saved if they would only accept Jesus as their savior and trust Him as their Lord. That word saved in the Greek means made whole, spiritually, mentally, physically, and emotionally, and financially, nothing missing, and nothing broken.

> And they sung a new song, saying, 'Thou art worthy to take the book, and to open the seals thereof: for thou wast slain, and hast redeemed us to God by thy blood out of every kindred, and tongue, and people, and nation'.
> —Revelations 5:9 (KJV)

Jesus paid the price for everyone, the whole world so that we could be saved from perishing with the world.

> And be not conformed to this world: but be ye transformed by the renewing of your mind, that ye may prove what is that good, and acceptable, and perfect, will of God.
> —Romans 12:2 (KJV)

We are instructed not to be conformed or shaped in mind or actions to be like this world. If it looks like a duck and quacks like a duck, and acts like a duck, it is a duck. If you look like the world, and talk like the world, and act like the world, you prove that you are of the world. If you speak the Word, and look like the Word, and act like the Word you are proving that you are of the Word, which is that good and acceptable and perfect will of God.

We want to step out in faith and live the life God designed. We live in the world, but we want to act like the Word, we want to look like and speak like the Word of God. So, what is up with the world? Why is it that God does not want us to conform to the world? Let us find out from the Word of God.

> Love not the world, neither the things that are in the world. If any man love the world, the love of the Father is not in him.
>
> —1 John 2:15 (KJV)

The world is now under the dominion of the kingdom of darkness ruled by Satan.

> For all that is in the world, the lust of the flesh, and the lust of the eyes, and the pride of life, is not of the Father, but is of the world.
>
> —1 John 2:16 (KJV)

1 John 2:16 tells us why God does not want us to conform to the world. All that is in the world is the lust of the flesh, the lust of the eyes and the pride of life. These three are not of the Father but are of the world and are still used by Satan today. They are called the Three-Fold Nature of

Temptation. With these three Satan is trying to steal the Word of God, which is absolute Truth, kill your faith in the true and living God and destroy your life. Those are all that are in the world and we do not want to conform to any of them.

> And the world passeth away, and the lust thereof: but he that doeth the will of God abideth for ever.
>
> —1 John 2:17 (KJV)

The world is perishing. It is passing away or dying. The lust found in the world is also passing away. That is the nature of lust. It must be repeated over and over again. The alcoholic must have a drink over and over. The drug addict must have the drug over and over. Satan wants the drug addict to overdose and try to make sure there is no one with Narcan (which reverses the effect of the drug) close by. The kleptomaniac must steal over and over. The nymphomaniac must have intimate relationships over and over. Why? Because the high passes away. The feeling of being satisfied, filled, or fulfilled, passes away.

David was a man after God's own heart, but he had a lust problem. He wanted Bathsheba and was willing to kill her husband, David's own soldier to have her. It was the lust of the eyes when he saw her bathing. It was the lust of the flesh when David put Bathsheba in his bed.

> All things are full of labour *(are wearisome)*;
> man cannot utter it: the eye is not satisfied
> with seeing, nor the ear filled with hearing.
>   —Ecclesiastes 1:8 (KJV)

David's son Solomon who wrote the books of Proverbs and Ecclesiastes was the wisest man in the world. He discovered that not living life according to the way of our Father in heaven designed it, was wearisome and meaningless. The lust of the eyes is apparent because according to Ecclesiastes 1:8 the eye never has enough of seeing. Solomon knew first-hand because of the number of wives and concubines he had (700 wives, 300 concubines.) He never had enough of seeing.

Look at the "woman at the well" in John 4 when Jesus asked her about her husband and she said she had no husband, Jesus told her she was right. He told her in fact, she had had five husbands and the man she was living with now was not her husband. She had a lust of the flesh problem. She needed man after man. When she came to the well Jesus asked her for water. Pick the story up there in John Chapter 4 and let us make a comparison of the things in the world compared to the things of God.

> Jesus answered and said unto her, 'If thou
> knewest the gift of God, and who it is that
> saith to thee, Give me to drink; thou wouldest

> have asked of Him, and He would have given
> thee living water.'
>
> —John 4:10 (KJV)

Jesus is speaking of spiritual water.

> [11] The woman saith unto him, 'Sir, thou hast
> nothing to draw with, and the well is deep:
> from whence then hast thou that living water?
> [12] Art thou greater than our father Jacob,
> which gave us the well, and drank thereof
> himself, and his children, and his cattle?'
> [13] Jesus answered and said unto her,
> 'Whosoever drinketh of this water shall thirst
> again.'
>
> —John 4:11-13 (KJV)

Water of the world will fill your thirst temporarily, but you must have it again. You will thirst again because the water is of the world and like everything else that temporarily fills in the world, will pass away.

> 'But whosoever drinketh of the water that I
> shall give him shall never thirst; but the water
> that I shall give him shall be in him a well of
> water springing up into everlasting life'.
>
> —John 4:14 (KJV)

That water that shall be inside man will be a well of water springing up into everlasting life is a type of the Word of God and the Spirit of God. The Word is Spirit, and it is life (John 6:63) The Word is the written Word in the Bible, and it is also Jesus's heavenly name. We see Him in action when the God said in Genesis 1, He said the Word, 'let there be light' and through the power of Holy Spirit there was light and so on. The Apostle John writes about it in the book of John.

> ¹ In the beginning was the Word, and the Word was with God, and the Word was God.
>
> ² The same was in the beginning with God.
>
> ³ All things were made by him; and without him was not anything made that was made.
>
> ⁴ In him was life; and the life was the light of men.
>
> ⁵ And the light shineth in darkness; and the darkness comprehended it not.
>
> —John 1:1-5 (KJV)

> And the Word was made flesh, and dwelt among us, (and we beheld his glory, the glory as of the only begotten of the Father,) full of grace and truth.
>
> —John 1:14 (KJV)

Holy Spirit is the third person of the Godhead. He speaks only truth and will testify or be a witness of Jesus Christ the Word of God. When we are born again, Holy Spirit comes to live inside us and is a witness to the Word of God. When we read and hear the Word it will renew our mind and increase our faith in God.

> But when the Comforter is come, whom I will send unto you from the Father, even the Spirit of truth, which proceedeth from the Father, he shall testify of me.
>
> —John 15:26 (KJV)

He will continually give you what you need, teach you what you need to know, comfort you in distress. He is an advocate for you with the Father. He will give you peace beyond all understanding, on and on. The well of water is the Word of God springing up into everlasting life. The water of the Word will cleanse and renew your mind. The blood of Jesus saves, cleanses, and regenerates your Spirit. Do not hunger or thirst after the world it will only give you temporary pleasures.

Our Heavenly Father wants us to hunger and thirst after righteousness. Believers are the righteousness of Christ. Hunger and thirst for the things of God, for the Word of God. God wants us to strive toward Christ's perfection. Jesus Christ only did the will of His Father. How can we know God's will? The Word of God is the will of God. So, hunger and thirst for the Word. We are in a spiritual battle for our very life. But get ready, we will win.

The steps of a good man are ordered by the Lord. Let us look at 5 points that will help us step out in faith and live the life God designed.

POINT 1. BE ANXIOUS FOR NOTHING.

This is easier said than done considering the world and the season we live in. But the Word of God gives us instructions and promises to help us in our daily walk.

> Be careful for nothing; but in everything by prayer and supplication with thanksgiving let your requests be made known unto God.
> —Philippians 4:6 (KJV)

> And Jesus looking upon them saith, 'With men it is impossible, but not with God: for with God all things are possible'.
> —Mark 10:27 (KJV)

Whatever is going on in your life, turn it over to God. Pray and ask God for direction. Locate a scripture to stand on. An example is if you are sick, if you have the Corona Virus, heart, liver, or lung disease, know that God is still in the healing business. Locate 1 Peter 2:24.

> Who his own self bare our sins in his own body on the tree, that we, being dead to sins,

> should live unto righteousness: by whose
> stripes ye were healed.
>
> —1 Peter 2:24 (KJV)

You stand on that scripture for your healing and pray, "Father your Word says that we were healed by the stripes Jesus bore on His own body over two thousand years ago. Today, the doctor's report says that I have diabetes, high blood pressure, cancer (or any other disease). I rebuke that in the Name of Jesus because the Word says by His stipes I am healed. If the Word says I am healed, I am healed. I thank you in advance and wait for the manifestation of my healing. In Jesus's Name I pray. Amen."

When your healing manifests the doctor will see it and tell you what to do next. Until then, follow the doctor's instructions. When I extract a tooth and suture the patient, that is my part. God heals the extraction site. Overtime, except for the space, you will never know a tooth was in that gum. God is a healer, the only healer.

Do not worry or be anxious about anything. Many are the afflictions of the righteous, but the Lord will deliver us out of them all (Psalms 34:19).

The important part to understand is what Jesus said in Mark 10:27, "with God." Jesus said it like this in John 15:5:

> I am the vine, ye are the branches: He that abideth *(continually abides)* in me, and I in him, the same bringeth forth much fruit: for without me ye can do nothing.
>
> —John 15:5 (KJV)

We will not have to worry when we abide in Jesus. The word abides in the Greek means to continue, to dwell, to be present, to remain, and to stand. (Strong 1822-1894) So, remain with Jesus and stand on the Word of God and we will not have to worry because "with God all things are possible." Wait on God. As we wait, He will renew our strength and we will mount up wings like the eagle. We will be able to run and not be weary walk and not faint. (Isaiah 40:31) Just continue to abide in Jesus.

POINT 2. LIFE'S RACE IS SET.

God has a plan for our entire life. The outcome is fixed, we win.

---

[1] Wherefore seeing we also are compassed about with so great a cloud of witnesses, let us lay aside every weight, and the sin which doth so easily beset us, and let us run with patience the race that is set before us,

[2] Looking unto Jesus the author and finisher of our faith; who for the joy that was set before Him endured the cross, despising the shame, and is set down at the right hand of the throne of God.

—Hebrews 12:1-2 (KJV)

The race begins as a child. That is the preparation time. We prepare our children for life by taking them to church weekly. There they develop the foundation, the start of a life-long relationship with God. They learn to read and study the Word of God. What they learn when young will develop as they mature in the Lord at each new level. Of course, this may require attending supplemental Bible studies for better understanding of spiritual or difficult concepts.

We prepare our children for living in the natural world by enrolling them in school. The foundational learning begins in pre-school and kindergarten. At each level new material is added in elementary, middle school, high school, and college. If they learn the material and get A's and B's building on each new level, they will be prepared for their life's work. Of course, this may require supplementing tutors for difficult subjects.

As our children watch current events every day on the news with us as they grow from a child, we can discuss the Christian response day by day to life, local, and world events. Not to mention by the time they get to High School and College they will know history, because they will have lived it, discussed, and understand it from a Christian perspective. This will help them as they research and write papers in English and other subjects.

All of this is a part of the race. Preparation, in the natural and in the spiritual. Why? Because we must live in the world. Since we are a part of the Kingdom of Heaven and we are assigned to be ambassadors, we need to be prepared to live, survive in, and reach the world teaching the Good News of Jesus, all the days of our lives. We also need to be prepared for the day when this life is over. We do that by running this race as a child of God and doing the work He has assigned for us to do. We look to Jesus the Author and Finisher of our faith, whose Word prepares us on how to live now and how to run God's race at the same time, as good and faithful servants.

The race ends at death, but the path is set. It will require patience to persevere and endure as we press towards that mark of the high calling (Philippians 3:14). There will be storms that will test our faith. There will be valleys that cast even a shadow of death (Psalms 23:4). But do not fear. That F.E.A.R. is False Evidence Appearing Real. Continue to walk through the valley in faith because God is with you. He will comfort you as you stretch toward that mark for the prize of the high calling in Christ Jesus. (Philippians 3:14) The prize is the victory of eternal life set for the overcomer and the more abundant life on earth now.

POINT 3. HAVE CONFIDENCE IN GOD.

Whatever your calling, whether you are a student, a person in one of the trades such as a carpenter, or a plumber; a person in a profession such as doctor or lawyer; a business owner; whether you are a worker in any job, have confidence in God. Pray for wisdom, revelation knowledge, and clarity in God's call on your life and the decisions you must make. Pray about what God's hope is for you and your future.

> For through him *(Jesus Christ)* we both have access by one Spirit unto the Father.
> —Ephesians 2:18 (KJV)

> [9] Who hath saved us, and called us with an holy calling, not according to our works, but according to His own purpose and grace, which was given us in Christ Jesus before the world began,
>
> [10] But is now made manifest by the appearing of our Savior Jesus Christ, who hath abolished death, and hath brought life and immortality to light through the gospel.
>
> —1 Timothy 1:9-10 (KJV)

> Being confident of this very thing, that he which hath begun a good work in you will perform it until the day of Jesus Christ.
>
> —Philippians 1:6 (KJV)

Our calling "is according to" God's "own purpose and grace" and was given to us by God in Christ Jesus. We think it was our own mental acuity and development, but God gave us the desires of our heart and the mental capacity to accomplish all we do. God started this work in us, and He will perform all that He wants us as His people to accomplish, until the day of Jesus Christ (The Day of the Lord, when Jesus comes back.)

Rest assured and be confident because God will not leave us or forsake us to be by ourselves or on our own. Just the opposite. God's plan for our lives is a good work. God gave us the blueprint before we were born, even in our mother's womb. The plans are complete, a finished work.

So, we can walk in confidence and have faith in God to do what He says He will do. God is not a man that he should lie (Numbers 23:19) He will finish, complete His purpose, His divine destiny in and for our lives.

Sometimes things will appear to go wrong or opposite to God's plan. But God!

> And we know that all things work together for good to them that love God, to them who are the called according to his purpose.
> —Romans 8:28 (KJV)

He has a master plan. He will take things that appear bad and turn them for our good. Why? Because God loves us and we "love God" and "are the called according to His purpose." Praise His holy Name.

POINT 4. WE ARE MORE THAN CONQUERORS.

> [35] Who shall separate us from the love of Christ? shall tribulation, or distress, or persecution, or famine, or nakedness, or peril, or sword?
> [36] As it is written, 'For thy sake we are killed all the day long; we are accounted as sheep for the slaughter.'
> [37] Nay, in all these things we are more than conquerors through him that loved us.
> —Romans 8:35-37 (KJV)

> *"A Psalm of David."* The LORD is my shepherd; I shall not want.
>
> —Psalm 23:1 (KJV)

> But thanks be to God, which giveth us the victory through our Lord Jesus Christ.
>
> —1 Corinthians 15:57 (KJV)

We are more than conquerors through Jesus Christ our Lord and Savior. He is the Good Shepherd that laid down His life for us (John 10:11). God has given us the victory through our Lord Jesus Christ. He now has dominion over the world (Romans 6:9-10). He now has the keys to hell and death (Revelation 1:18). We have a King who is King of Kings and Lord of Lords (Revelation 17:14). He owns the earth and they that dwell therein (Psalms 24:1). He wants to take care of us which is why the 23rd Psalm says the LORD is my shepherd (Psalms 23:1). We are sheep, unable to take care of ourselves or bear any burden. But the LORD being our shepherd means I shall not want. King David said it like this, "I have never seen the righteous forsaken nor his seed begging bread" (Psalms 37:25). We are in a spiritual war and we will be victorious "through our Lord Jesus Christ" (1 Corinthians 15:57).

POINT 5. GREATER IS HE THAT IS IN YOU

Yes, I know the Word says we will be victorious, but look at all the problems, all the chaos in the world. It appears life is getting harder not easier. Now we have the Corona Virus, and it is raging across the country and the world. People are losing their jobs, and companies are closing. How are we going to win with all that? When that is over there will be something else.

> Ye are of God, little children, and have overcome them: because greater is he that is in you, than he that is in the world.
> —1 John 4:4 (KJV)

When we accept Jesus as Lord and Savior, Holy Spirit comes to live in us. Holy Spirit is God, the third part of the Godhead with the Father and Son. Holy Spirit raised Jesus from the dead. If He is that powerful and He lives in us, teaching us, helping us, comforting us and more, that is how we can have the victory. Greater is He (Holy Spirit) that is in us, leading us, guiding us, interceding for us, than he (Satan) that is in the world.

FINALLY

Step out in faith. Faith is the victory that overcomes the world. Stay in the Word, meditate on it day and night. Walk in victory, stepping as God guides, one foot in front of another. Our steps are ordained, ordered by the Lord. Be strong in the Lord and the power of His might (Ephesians 6:10). The joy of the Lord is our strength (Nehemiah 8:10). We will step out in faith and endure until the end.

We must be diligent to the call that God has on our life. We have indeed been chosen to walk in our path. We must be diligent throughout our entire life to follow where God leads us.

> Wherefore the rather, brethren, give diligence to make your calling and election sure: for if ye do these things, ye shall never fall (KJV).
> —2 Peter 1:10 (KJV)

If we do these things, we will not fail.

> I will praise thee; for I am fearfully and wonderfully made: marvellous are thy works; and that my soul knoweth right well.
> —Psalms 139:14 (KJV)

We are fearfully and wonderfully made or designed. That means you are fantastic in God's eyes. Think of all your attributes, your profession, your talent(s), every good and perfect gift is from above (James 1:17). That means that God has made you and given you everything you need to achieve, succeed, and survive in this world. If you follow God and be a doer of the word, you will never fail. So, while we wait for "The End", we must step out in faith and live the life God designed.

BIBLIOGRAPHY

Bullinger, E. W. 1967. Number In Scripture: It's Supernatural Design and Spiritual Significance. Grand Rapids: Kregel Publications.

Byrd, Deborah. 2019. Today in science: The Chelyabinsk meteor. February 15. Accessed March 11, 2020. https://earthsky.org/space/meteor-asteroid-chelyabinsk-russia-feb-15-2013.

Conner, Kevin J. 1992. "Interpreting the Symbols and Types." In Interpreting the Symbols and Types, by Kevin J. Conner, 125-177. Portland: City Bible Publishing.

Garcia, Anne T. 2014. "From The Hidden Final Edition." In From The Hidden Final Edition, by Anne T. Garcia, 19-21. Maitland: Xulon Press.

Johnston, Robert D. 1990. "Numbers in the Bible." In Numbers in the Bible God's Design in Biblical Numerology, by Robert D Johnston, 67-69. Grand Rapids: Kregel Publications.

LaHaye, Tim, and Thomas Ice. 2001. Charting the End Times. Eugene: Harvest House Publishers.

LaHaye, Tim, Jerry B Jenkins, and Alan B McElroy. 2000. Left Behind The Movie. DVD. Directed by Vic Sarin.

Produced by Peter Executive Producers: Lalonde, Paul LaLonde, Bobby Neutz, Ron. Producers: LaLonde, Peter Booth, Paul LaLonde, Joe Goodman and Ralph Winter. Performed by Kirk Cameron, Brad Johnson, Chelsea Noble, Clarence Gilyard, Janaya Stephens, Colin Fox and Gordon Currie.

Lalonde, Paul, and John Patus. 2002. Left Behind II: Tribulation Force. DVD. Directed by Bill Corcoran. Produced by Ron Executive Producers: Booth, Peter Lalonde, Edwin Ng and Nicholas D. Producer: Tabarrok. Performed by Kirk Cameron, Brad Johnson, Chelsea Noble, Clarence Gilyard and Currie Gordon.

MacArthur, John F. 2007. Because the Time is Near: John MacArthur Explains the Book of Revelation. Chicago: Moody Publishers.

Monroe, Miles. 2010. "Rediscovering the Kingdom." In Rediscovering the Kingdom, by Miles Monroe, 28-40. Shippensburg: Destiny Image Publishers, Inc.

Smith, Carol, Rachael Phillips, and Ellyn Sanna. 2011. "Women of the Bible, A Visual Guide To Their Lives, Loves And Legacy." In Women of the Bible, A Visual Guide To Their Lives, Loves And Legacy, by Carol Smith, Rachael Phillips and Ellyn Sanna, 67-76. Uhrichsville: Barbour Publishing, Inc.

Stephan Blinn, Hollis Barton, John Fasano, Stephan Blinn. 2001. Meggido: The Omega Code 2. Directed by Brian Trenchard-Smith. Produced by Lawrence Mortorff, Richard J. Cook Matthew Crouch and Executive Producer Paul Crouch. Performed by Michael Biehn Michael York.

Strong, James. 1822-1894. The New Strong's Exhaustive Concordance of the Bible. Nashville, Atlanta, London, Vancouver: Thomas Nelson Publishers.

U.S. Geological Survey - Earthquake Hazards Program. n.d. 1906 Marked the Dawn of the Scientific Revolution. Accessed March 8, 2020. https://earthquake.usgs. gov/earthquakes/events/1906calif/18april/revolution. php.

Vocabulary.com. n.d. asteroid. Accessed March 11, 2020. https://www.vocabulary.com/dictionary/asteroid.

ABOUT THE AUTHOR

Dr. Monoseta C. Burwell is a wife, a mother, an Oral/Maxillofacial Surgeon with a General Dental Practice, and an instructor at her newest venture, the Dental Assistant Academy, LLC. She is also a retired Pastor of Light of the World Christian Center after 17.5 years, where her husband Pastor Bruce D. Burwell was the Senior Pastor. Dr. Burwell and her husband still minister the Word when asked to preach at various churches across the country.

If you ask her about this book, she will tell you God wrote it. With her busy schedule, there is no other way possible. He creates the space in her week to accomplish all that He wants to accomplish through her. With that said, the book answers all the questions Dr. Burwell had about the end-times, and she wanted to share the information with the world. It is her hope that everyone who is touched by this book will use it to share the Good News of Jesus Christ, help to build the Kingdom of God, and prepare for the end of time.

Dr. Monoseta C Burwell can be contacted at:

drmcburwell@gmail.com

CPSIA information can be obtained
at www.ICGtesting.com
Printed in the USA
LVHW010323180621
690506LV00012B/543